CHICKEN LIPS, SNAKE LEGS, & JESUS

Stories of Humor & Hope For Life's Journey

WALKER MOORE

Kudos From The Coop

"Walker Moore has a gift. He writes about valuable lessons couched in common experiences with a spiritual tone and a great sense of humor." —Charles Biggs, editor/publisher, Tulsa Beacon

"Another 'must-have' from Walker Moore, talented author, gifted evangelist, and storyteller. Walker will have you laughing, crying, and spiritually convicted all in the same paragraph." —Larry Bodden, Roy, Utah

"Walker Moore is skilled at using humor to communicate eternal truth while sharing the examples of God's deep love and desire for all people to come to know Him. You will laugh and be challenged to step up to what God has called us to do." —Penny Blalock, Kirksville, Missouri

"You will always get a laugh and learn a biblical truth that can transform your life when reading one of Walker's books. I've never regretted reading his writings, and neither will you." —April Cole, children's pastor, First United Methodist, Odessa, Texas

"Walker is a guy who knows how to turn the ordinary into the extraordinary just by walking with Jesus. If you want to be compelled to reach the next level in your faith, follow him." —Becky Dietz, Double Honor Ministries

"Walker will give you insights to biblical principles from a creative but factual perspective. He will help you see that God loves you deeply." —Phil Dietz, community pastor, Evergreen Baptist Church, Bixby, Oklahoma

"Walker Moore has been on mission adventures for four decades. In this book, you will go with him on a journey dotting the globe to experience the unusual, the humorous, and the inspiring. Walker will show you how doing 'Jesus ministry' is the adventure of a lifetime that echoes into eternity." —Timbo Fowler, pastor, Church by the Fort, Killeen, Texas

"Walker uses his unique blend of humor through real-life-stories to produce handles from which we can understand, apply, and carry truth." —Brent Higgins, associate pastor, Parkview Baptist Church, Tulsa, Oklahoma

"Through the entertaining adventures of Walker Moore, this book shares the power and truth of a life lived for Jesus. As you read these stories, enjoy a laugh and see a love where lives are impacted for eternity." —Angela Hudgins, minister to youth, Highland Terrace Baptist Church, Greenville, Texas

"Jesus ministry is intentional and is 24/7—two of the many thing I have learned from Walker Moore. Through his life, you will see these elements live through this book that will challenge, equip, and encourage you to join in God's great adventures." —Mike Lehew, executive director, Mobile Missions Network, Sapulpa, Oklahoma

"Walker Moore always reaches into his pantry of heartwarming anecdotes, illustrations, and wisdom to create the perfect recipe to delight, challenge, and inspire the reader." —Bob Nigh, Historical Secretary, Baptist General Convention of Oklahoma

"The teachings of Walker Moore have impacted me to have a heartbeat of obedience." —Greg Sweatt, pastor, Phoenix Community, Buford, Georgia

"Walker is the best at using humor, wisdom, and insights in a compelling way that will change your life and the lives of those you love the most." —Corey Webb, executive/community pastor, Crosspoint Fellowship, San Antonio, Texas

CHICKEN LIPS, SNAKE LEGS, & JESUS

Stories of Humor & Hope For Life's Journey

WALKER MOORE

Published by DustJacket
P.O. Box 721243
Oklahoma City, OK
www.dustjacket.com

Printed in the United States of America
Library of Congress Cataloging-in-Publication Data

Moore, Walker.
    Chicken Lips, Snake Legs, and Jesus
    p.   cm.
ISBN: 978-1-947671-19-5

Dedicated to Titus the Honorable and Cohen the Goodhearted, the only two boys who call me Poppy.

Contents

Acknowledgments

A number of people have made this publication possible, of whom I am the least.

I would like to thank the Baptist Messenger of Oklahoma for asking me so long ago to write this column. They asked me to fill in until they could find a full-time writer. Twenty years and one thousand articles later, I am still going.

For this book, we have chosen some of the best stories of humor and hope. Selecting just these few was a difficult process; but don't worry, there is another book coming.

I would like to thank Marti Pieper. I will never be able to thank her enough for all the years she has edited, corrected, and polished each one of these articles. Marti, I could not have had a better publishing partner than you.

I would like to thank Mark Combs, who has designed the cover, formatted this book, and prayed and prodded me along. But Mark has done more than that. He was also part of the team that helped me carry the cross up Mount Kilimanjaro. Mark, we are forever brothers, connected at the cross.

I would like to thank Chris Robinette, who has guided me over the years through the maze of the publishing industry. Without you, this book would still be sitting in a drawer.

I would like to thank my family: my wife, Cathy; my sons, Jeremiah and Caleb; my daughters-in-love, Erin and Adrian; and of course those two little boys who call me Poppy. It is my family who makes life interesting and provides good writing material. I love you all.

But I am most grateful to you, my readers, who have kept reading these stories over the past twenty years. As you read and reread them, may God warm your heart and tickle your funny bone.

Your servant,

Walker Moore

Foreword

Since 1998, Walker Moore has delighted tens of thousands of Baptist Messenger readers in Oklahoma and around the world with his weekly writings. Walker, in many ways, is a combination of the admirable qualities we see in noteworthy men like Paul Harvey, Billy Graham, Will Rogers, and the fictional Forrest Gump.

Let me explain. Like Paul Harvey, Walker Moore is a master storyteller who engages the heart of his readers. Like Dr. Graham, Walker has shared the gospel both one-on-one and in large-group settings with fire and passion. Like Will Rogers, Walker displays an amazing and unforgettable sense of humor. His wit and wisdom are the most remarkable I have seen. And God seems to place Walker, like a super-smart version of the movie character Forrest Gump, in the midst of incredible moments and circumstances where he makes a lasting impact.

I am thrilled that Walker has assembled this collection

of writings. Within the pages of Chicken Lips, Snake Legs & Jesus, you will find one-of-a-kind, unforgettable stories.

Through Walker's experiences, you will discover how the phrase "Bob Loves You" used in another country reveals God's love. You will read a heart-moving account about a young "girl in a yellow dress" whose smile shows the glory of God. Through a hilarious account, you'll discover how to be Savior-centered and live for an Audience of One.

You'll learn that, yes, there are really are some dumb questions in life, but they can often point us to deeper truths. And above all, you will see that you—yes, you right there—are both a child of the King and Jesus's favorite child.

I know the stories of humor and hope contained in this collection by Walker Moore will make every person who reads them laugh, cry, and find wisdom godly wisdom.

Brian Hobbs

Editor, Oklahoma Baptist Messenger

Chicken Lips,
Snake Legs & Jesus

There is a fine line between creative and crazy. I am still trying to determine which category I fall into. I have been labeled both.

One of my creative friends, who shall remain nameless, told me a story he now claims he never told. I guess this will either protect the innocent or the guilty, whichever one applies. It had to do with one of those non-brand name scraggly little stores with a couple of gas pumps out front. Not only did this store carry your normal sundries like milk, eggs, and bread, but it also sold fried chicken.

Now, I am not the type of person whose first thought is to run to a gas station when my wife calls and asks me to bring home fried chicken.

I am sure gas stations make chicken just as good as any colonel from Kentucky, but that thought never occurs to me. And the people who owned this store must have realized there were lots of folks like me. The demand for their fried chicken was at best slow and at worst sparse. Wanting to create more traffic, they decided to change the marquee and advertise "Today's Special: World's Best Fried Chicken Lips: $1.25/lb."

I thought this was humorous, but did you know there are people in this world who are interested in eating chicken lips? The cars began to pull into that convenience store for the sole purpose of trying a pound of its world-class fried chicken lips. The store's owner (who shall still remain nameless) announced to the customers that he was terribly sorry, "We've just sold out."

If they had only come a few minutes earlier, he assured them, they could have tried some. But the good news was he still had some fresh-cooked legs, breasts, wings, and thighs. Instead of going home empty-handed, they all walked out with sacks of every part of the chicken except its lips.

By this time, business was booming. People came from far and near to try the "World's Best Fried Chicken Lips."

Wanting to take his business to the next level, the owner came up with a second brilliant marketing idea. He would offer a two-meat platter with fries. Now, he was selling a "Fried Chicken Lips and Snake Legs Combo." If you thought the people clamored for fried chicken lips, you should have seen the crowd that showed up for the snake legs. And as always, the owner gave them the same story about having just sold out.

Now, I'm not sure about the truth of this story, even though I heard it from a friend who heard it from the friend of a friend. But it does remind me a lot of this old world.

People are gullible. A new chicken lips or snake legs salesman comes to town on a regular basis, touting the answer to your problem. There's just one issue: You didn't know you had a problem until he showed up. And people will line up, shelling out their hard-earned money for something that isn't real.

As it turns out, many of these chicken lips/snake legs types are out to sell you some form of religion. They always have some special gimmick and prey on others' hopelessness. "You send us just one dollar and have enough faith, and guess what God will do? He'll return it to you tenfold." And people line up to give their dollars, hoping something good will happen. But when they come to collect on the promise, guess what? The salesman is fresh out.

That's one of the reasons God sent his Son, Jesus: So we could know the truth, the real truth.

Jesus didn't come to tout a new religion; what He wanted was a relationship.

A relationship with you. That's why He had to die on a cross to take away the sin barrier. And now He proclaims, "'I am the way and the truth and the life. No one comes to the Father except through me'" (John 14:6).

When you pull in to check out Jesus, you won't get an "I'm sorry, we just sold out" speech. Instead, you'll hear Him say, "Come to me, all who are weary and burdened, and I will give you rest" (Matt. 11:28). And His marquee always reads the same: "Whoever believes in Me shall have: Life, peace, hope, direction, destiny, love . . ."

And that beats chicken lips or snake legs every time.

Dream On

I have confessed before that I am a dreamer. Being this type of person has its ups and downs. You're always looking forward to something, but you'll never get to see all your dreams fulfilled.

There are several things I would love to do. I would like to take my wife to Paris and spend a night at the Shangri-La Hotel. She has never been to Paris, but I have. A couple of times, I had a layover of a few hours there before the night train headed out to Budapest. While waiting, I would walk the streets to experience the sights and sounds. On one of these walkabouts, I happened upon the Shangri-La Hotel. The first time I saw it, I said to myself, "One of these days, I'm going to bring my wife here." There are more exquisite hotels in Paris, but the name Shangri-La intrigues me.

In our journey, my wife and I have slept in some of the worst places in the world.

I remember getting sick in the forest of Ukraine when it had rained nonstop for two weeks and was bitterly cold. I was living in a little concrete building about the size of a storage shed. It had no heat, no running water, and no furniture, just a single mattress. And I wasn't the only one using the mattress. It was full of varmints, and I could feel them moving around whenever I tried to sleep.

When I walk by an opulent place like the Shangri-La, I wonder what it would be like to spend a night there. I bet there are no varmints living in their mattresses. Are the sheets satin? I bet I couldn't even pronounce the name of the soap. It's no doubt filled with rich lanolin and oils infused with exotic perfume. I'm sure guests are all treated like royalty. And the food? I imagine the Shangri-La employs only renowned chefs who see cooking more as art than order, each course more decadent than the one before it.

I have looked online at the images of this hotel. It has one of the top ten indoor swimming pools in the world. And the reviews say the photos don't do it justice. I would like to walk into the foyer (pronounced with a French accent, "foi-yay," not like a Baptist, "foy-yer") with my wife on my arm. No matter how beautiful the architecture, she would be the most stunning thing in the hotel. On her wrist would be the little diamond bracelet I bought her a long time ago. It isn't fancy, but she does wear it well.

Yes, if any woman deserves to have something nice done for her, it's this one. While other couples were building a bigger house and buying a boat, she was cooking for hundreds of people over a single hot plate in Mexico while enduring extreme heat and long hours. While our peers were building their nest eggs, she was sleeping on all-night trains with strangers, helping lead a group of students to towns that had never heard the gospel. Can you see why I dream of doing something special for her? She is royalty, not because she met a handsome prince but because her Father is a King. Yes, I am married to the daughter of the King of kings.

God's intention when He designed us as men was that we reflect His image and character.

But because of the Fall, we seldom do. And the people who pay the price for our failure to live the way the Master

Designer planned are our family members: our wives, our children and even ourselves. When our families look into our eyes, it should be the same as looking into God's eyes. They should know that they are fearfully and wonderfully made, that they are individuals with worth and value. That way, they don't have to go running off to the wrong places to find their worth. They already have it.

One of these days, my wife's Heavenly Father will take her back home to the palace. "And if I go and prepare a place for you, I will come back and take you to be with me that you also may be where I am" (John14:3). I've read about this place Jesus has prepared for us. It has streets of gold; there is no darkness, sickness, or sorrow. The food will be like nothing we've ever seen before. And its grandeur will make the Shangri-La of Paris look like a condemned building.

I guess I do reflect my Father's love in a small way. I love my wife and want the best for her. Our Heavenly Father loves us, and He has gone ahead to prepare the best for us: heaven.

Going Blind

As I write this, I'm in Mexico with a group of students doing mission work. Forty-nine of us are jammed together in a church, living, eating, and serving God together.

The difference between my age and the students' is getting increasingly wide. One of them asked me how old I was, and I told her "Sixty-two."

"Wow! You're older than my grandparents!" she said, then caught herself and added, "Oh! But you look and act younger than they do." Good try.

I realize I'm not as young as I used to be. The eye doctor tells me I have the beginning of cataracts, and the gleam in my eyes now comes from the sun hitting my bifocals. When I see a quarter on the floor, it isn't worth the effort to bend over and pick it up. My wife complains that I keep the volume on the television uncomfortably loud. But I'm not sure how she knows. She's getting as deaf as I am.

Still, I don't mind getting older. I've learned there are a number of perks. Your supply of brain cells is finally down to a manageable size. Your secrets are safe with your friends, because they can't remember them either. You can sing along with elevator music. You don't need a twenty-year guarantee for the things you buy. Your joints are more accurate at predicting the weather than the local meteorologist. You can eat dinner out and still be home for the five o'clock news, and there is nothing left to learn the hard way.

But this morning, I had a scare. I got up at six o'clock to do my quiet time, reading my Bible and meditating upon its meaning. I didn't want to disturb the students, so I reached over in the dark, put on my glasses, and opened my Kindle (which is backlit) to read the Scriptures. Sometimes my eyes take a few minutes to adjust first thing in the morning. But today, nothing looked right.

I squinted, hoping things would improve, but the blurriness only got worse. I held the Kindle farther away from my face. Sometimes that helps, but this time, it didn't work.

I finally adjusted the font size to the largest setting, the size of a Volkswagen Beetle.

It was so big the person in the next county could read it. But even at that size, the type was blurry. I kept reading, figuring sooner or later my sight would snap back into focus. I spent an hour trying to make out the fuzzy letters, and when my eyes grew tired, I lay back down on my cot, covered my eyes with my arm and started praying.

There are several kinds of prayers. There is the one that comes off the top of your head when you are asked to bless the meal at Uncle Albert's house, and then there is the one that comes from somewhere deep inside as you cry out to God. This prayer was the latter; I needed God to heal my eyes. How could I make it through the day or even drive in Mexico if everything was out of focus? As I lay there for some time, praying, I heard one of our leaders ask, "Has anybody seen my glasses?" I didn't want to stop praying, but a thought popped into my mind. *Could it be?*

Interrupting one of the greatest prayers for healing ever, I slowly raised my arm and pulled off my glasses. Upon close examination, I realized they weren't mine after all. Somehow in the darkness I had reached over and picked up the wrong glasses. I gave them back, put on my own pair, and my vision was instantly healed.

But I am not the only one who has ever had blurred vision. When it comes to spiritual things, many people have a hard time seeing the hand of God. You look at life through television, magazines, circumstances, or even through the eyes of others. You're convinced God doesn't care and has forsaken you.

I suggest you change your glasses.

Look at your life through the lens that will give you clarity: the Word of God.

As you search His Word, ask God to give you wisdom. James 1:5 says, "If any of you lacks wisdom, you should ask God, who gives generously to all without finding fault." Next, be prepared for Him to help you see clearly: "Now then, stand still and see this great thing the Lord is about to do before your eyes!" (1 Sam. 12:16).

Reading the Bible is a great way to bring things into focus—as long as you wear the right glasses.

Cow Hair

This year, three farmers at the Ohio State Fair were disqualified for the discovery that their cows wore hairpieces. According to the *Akron Beacon Journal*, Kreg Krebs, his brother Kenneth, and Scott Long were arrested for tampering with two Holstein cows. (I didn't even know cows could be tampered with.) These three men were accused of gluing and painting hairpieces on the backs of their cows to give them a straighter back, thus enhancing the cows' appearance in the show ring.

Now, you might think this was odd, but then the state inspectors from the fair were interviewed, they said cases like this are not "highly unusual."

"It is the first time we have collected enough evidence to prosecute," reported the inspectors. (I don't know how many hairpieces you need to have enough evidence, but it seems to me it wouldn't take many.)

These cows were caught as the inspectors ran their hands over the animals looking for illegal fitting and grooming. Consequently, the two cows were disqualified from the state fair (I tend to believe that these cows had no idea they were wearing hairpieces, compliments of their owners, and they should in no way have been penalized) and the men were ordered to forfeit all winnings.

I had two reactions when I read this story. One, it tickled my funny bone. Can you imagine three farmers dressed in overalls and boots wandering around the women's area of some department store, looking for wigs and hairpieces for their cows? I wondered what they said to the salesperson who asked, "May I help you with something?"

> "Yes, can you help us find some cheap, coarse-looking hairpieces? We'd prefer white with black spots."

"Are these for your wives?"

"Oh, no, they're not for our wives. We need them for someone special—our cows."

I would love to have seen the reaction on the salesperson's face. And if she were on her toes, she would probably have shown them several shades of lipstick to complement the hairpieces.

What the judge really should have done was order the men to wear the cow's hairpieces themselves until the next state fair. Then they would have understood the humiliation they brought on these two "all-beef patties."

> But the farmers' actions didn't surprise me; it's just another story about winning at all costs.

Our society has come to the idea that as long as we come out on top, it doesn't matter how we get there. And this is a story as old as mankind: "'You will not certainly die,' the serpent said to the woman. 'For God knows that when you eat from it your eyes will be opened, and you will be like God, knowing good and evil'" (Gen. 3:4, 5).

Yes, even in the beginning, we humans have wanted to be on the top, number one. That's what makes Jesus' message so radical. It's about denying yourself, becoming a servant, giving your life for another. He knew if we were

31

left to our own ways, we would end up putting hairpieces on cows to win a contest. But Jesus has a better way for us, and it is the road less traveled.

We might not win first place in this world, but we will be number one in His eyes. And if we do what He tells us, when we face the eternal judgment, He will pronounce to us, "Well done, thou good and faithful servant." And that, my friend, is better than any state fair ribbon.

I have found a hair in my hamburger once, maybe even twice. I thought they were human hairs but now I am wondering if they were part of the cow's hairpiece.

Goofy Tales

If I had to choose the Disney character that best represented me, Goofy would suit just fine. He's good-natured, doesn't take anything too seriously, make jokes, is slightly clumsy and says, "Yuk, yuk" when he gets tickled. He may not be the sharpest crayon in the box, but his heart is bigger than all outdoors. Everybody loves Goofy.

I was picking up students from the airport the other day when Melanie, one of our summer staffers, asked what I'd learned after 40 years of working with students. I thought for a second and said, "There's a little bit of Goofy in all of us."

> You see, every one of us makes Goofy mistakes.

I don't care how careful, smart or sophisticated you are. Sooner or later, you'll make one. One summer, I was living in Budapest, where they speak Hungarian, one of the most difficult languages in the world. I had run out of hairspray and went to the drugstore to buy another can.

This was the best hairspray I'd ever seen. Even if a hurricane-strength wind blew, it would keep my hair in place.

I bragged to the Hungarians about their wonderful product. And that's when I found out it wasn't hairspray, but deodorant. Hey, at least my head didn't sweat. Remember? We all make Goofy mistakes.

We've all asked a Goofy question, too. I could make a list as long as my arm of the Goofy questions I've heard while taking students around the world. "What country is France in?" asked one. While we were serving in Africa, another student asked me, "Are we looking at the other side of the moon?"

I've also heard, "Why are there so many foreigners in this country?" Actually, we're the foreigners here.

"Do we need our bathing suits when we go swimming?" I guess swimming suits are optional in some countries, but yes, we'll wear ours.

"What time does the eight o'clock train come?" Now, that's a tough one. "If it's on time, eight o'clock."

"How many dollars does it take to buy this [fill in the blank])?" Since the store in this country doesn't take dollars, the answer is "None."

You can add your own Goofy questions, but at some point, we've all asked at least one.

If you've ever served cross-culturally, you've had a Goofy international moment, too. When I was in China, I didn't know cleaning your plate was considered bad manners. All my life, my parents taught me to clean my plate because "People are starving in China."

The first few days I was there, I offended everyone. I worked too hard to clean my plate, and they kept giving me more and more food. I should have left a little to indicate I was full and they had given me more than enough to eat. Eight pounds later, I learned this lesson.

One of our student missionaries once got the Spanish words for "sin" and "fish" mixed up (they sound almost the same). The Mexican church was shocked when she gave her testimony. "Jesus died for your fish" she told them. "And if you let Him, He will take your fish as far as the east is from the west and bury it in the deepest sea."

Sooner or later, everyone will also have a Goofy God-moment.

This happened to me just the other day. I was in a college cafeteria and asked the director of the kitchen to come out to meet our students. Next, I asked if he would allow me to pray for him. Yes, it was awkward, but he let me do it. In the middle of my prayer, I felt led to start praying for his four children. I asked God specifically to put a hedge of protection around them, to watch over them.

The man didn't know why I was praying for his family, but later, he came and thanked me. I had no idea that the same week, his four-year-old daughter fell into a neighbor's pool, and they found her unresponsive. They called 911 and rushed her to the hospital, but it wasn't looking good. The doctors had given them very little hope when she suddenly made a miraculous recovery, stunning the medical team.

"The turnaround happened at the exact time you were praying for God to protect my children," he said. When I was praying, it felt Goofy, but it turned out to be a Goofy God-moment.

Yes, we all have a Goofy gene. But the good news is God loves the Goofys of the world and has plans for our lives: "'For I know the plans I have for you,' declares the LORD, 'plans to prosper you and not to harm you, plans to give you hope and a future'" (Jer. 29:11). There's nothing Goofy about that.

Or is there?

Jesus is Enough

I had just moved to Hannibal, Missouri, to attend Hannibal-LaGrange College. I didn't know anyone there, and I wasn't sure of my living arrangements, but I knew Jesus was enough.

I moved into a dormitory room and soon realized that dorm life and studying don't necessarily go together. I was walking through downtown Hannibal, contemplating what to do, when a man I didn't know approached and asked if I was Walker Moore. When I said yes, he told me, "I have a two-story house I would like you to live in. You won't have to pay anything; just keep up the front yard."

I checked it out, and the front yard was very small. Just as it says in the Bible, "And my God will meet all your needs according to the riches of his glory in Christ Jesus" (Phil. 4:19).

That house became a place of ministry as other men

moved in for me to disciple. But one day, we ran out of food.

Some of the guys were on parole and offered to go into town to steal some food for us.

But I asked them to wait upon the Lord for at least twenty-four hours.

I went out to the little country church I served and got on my knees, praising and thanking God for all the things He had done. When I finished, I locked the church door, walked out to my van, and opened it. A small package fell to the ground. I picked it up and discovered it was rock-hard and cold as ice. I held it under the dome light to read the print on the package: "Chuck Roast."

While I was inside the church praying, someone had filled my van with meats, vegetables, canned goods and a block of cheese. To this day, I don't know the identity of this angel of kindness. But again, God came through: "And my God will meet all your needs according to the riches of his glory in Christ Jesus" (Phil. 4:19).

Later, I needed a car—nothing fancy, just something to

get me from point A to point B. One Sunday night, I went to the altar after the message and lay on the steps, asking God to help me find a car. I had told no one else of my need.

I felt a hand on my shoulder, and a man leaned down and whispered, "I thought you might need this." He laid a set of car keys next to me.

After the service, I went over and asked him, "How did you know I needed a car?"

"I bought a new car and was going to trade this one, but the dealership gave me such a ridiculously low price, I thought it would be better to give it to an individual than to the dealership," he said. "Your name came to mind."

I drove that orange Honda Civic for years. Once again, God met my need: "And my God will meet all your needs according to the riches of his glory in Christ Jesus" (Phil. 4:19).

One Christmas morning, I had to travel from Hannibal to Dallas. I had one more semester of school and had just gotten married. I was now taking care of two houses, and my little country church paid me fifty dollars a week. Like most college students, I was barely making it.

Coming back from Dallas, I ran out of gas on Turner

Turnpike between Oklahoma City and Tulsa, and I sat on the side of the road at 3 a.m. I got on my CB radio and asked if anyone knew where the nearest FINA gasoline station was. My mother had given me a FINA credit card on my wedding night and told me to use it when I was in trouble. Since I had no cash left in my wallet, I thought this situation would qualify.

A truck driver came on, laughing. "There's no FINA around for hundreds of miles," he said. "But if you're still on the side of the road when I come by, I'll see if I can help." I prayed and prayed.

Soon, I heard the squealing brakes of a semi as the truck pulled up next to my van. It was a gasoline truck, and the driver, who had talked to me over the CB radio, asked how much I wanted.

"Fill 'er up!" I said, hoping he would take a FINA card. He finished, refusing to take any payment at all. He climbed into his cab and drove off.

Yet again, God had shown Himself strong.

After following Jesus for more than fifty years, I can tell you that it's still true: Jesus is enough.

Steak and Shake

I can remember the day—August 4—but not the
year. All I know is that my sons were in elementary
school. Somehow, the older I get, the more those years
get confused. I will say to Jeremiah or Caleb, "Do you
remember when you hit a home run in the third grade?"
and he will say, "No, Dad, it was a double, and I was in
the seventh grade." I've learned to just start out with
"Remember when. . . ?" and let my boys fill in the details.

I'm sure I remember the exact day because it was the
birthday of Jeremiah, my oldest son. I felt bad for him.
We were driving the eight hours from Grandma's house in
Hannibal, Missouri, all the way home to Tulsa. No child
should spend his birthday in the back seat of a car. How
could I make this day special?

As we approached Springfield, I remembered a Steak
and Shake restaurant there.

If I knew anything about Jeremiah, I knew he loved meat. As a boy, I saw an episode of Mutual of Omaha's Wild Kingdom that featured footage of a cow wading into a river. Within ten seconds, a school of piranhas ate the poor animal clear to the bone. Watching Jeremiah eat meat brought back that episode—in living color.

I said to him, "Do you know what a man should have on his birthday?"

His eyes grew huge. "No, Daddy, what?"

"A man needs a steak. A big, juicy steak. That's what a man should have on his birthday."

I could sense the wheels spinning inside his little head: *It's my birthday. I am a man. That means I should have steak today.*

My next words made the wheels go even faster. "That's not all, Jeremiah. Do you know what else a man should have?"

"What's that, Daddy?"

"A shake. A thick chocolate shake to wash down that steak. That is what a man needs on his birthday: a steak and a shake."

By now, his little wheels were turning double-time. The only thing Jeremiah consumed faster than meat was chocolate. Once again, I could see his thoughts: *Today is my birthday. I am a man. I should celebrate with a steak and a shake.*

I spoke once again. "Jeremiah, would you do me a favor? I need to keep my eyes on the road. Could you watch for a place that serves steaks and shakes?"

At this point, Jeremiah was leaning over the back seat, straining to find such a place. I knew that in a mile or so, we would reach a sign with directions to the Steak and Shake restaurant. Every fifteen seconds I would ask, "Have you found anything yet?" and he would shake his head, "No."

It's a good thing I anticipated the sign. When Jeremiah caught sight of it, he screamed at the top of his lungs, "Look, Dad—a place that sells steaks and shakes!"

"Good! Let's go there and celebrate your birthday!"

Jeremiah is now thirty years old. Recently, he asked me, "Dad, you remember when we ate at Steak and Shake for my birthday?"

Of course, I did—although I'm glad he didn't press me about the year. "Dad, what you did—that was pretty cool."

I smiled.

Isn't that what our heavenly Father does?

He plants dreams, desires, and hopes into His children's minds and hearts.

He knows if we keep looking ahead, we will soon discover the place where He brings fulfillment.

Even if it has nothing to do with a shake or a steak.

Significance— and Creamed Corn

I reached a mile marker this week, and it has hit me hard. I tried to convince the government I wasn't old enough, but last week, they made me apply for Medicare.

First of all, I'm not sure who this Medi is and whether she really does care. Second, everyone in the world seems to know I'm in this season of life. I've received a boatload of mail, all saying, "Congratulations, old man! You are turning sixty-five soon, and you know what that means. . ."

> Yes, my body is still the temple of God, but my steeple is beginning to droop.

To be honest, I'm concerned that my days of having a significant role in life are coming to a close. I've seen far too many people my age and older who have given up and spend their time just puttering around.

Maybe we all go through this process, but this side of heaven, I want to do more than mark time. I like what Chuck Norris's mom, Wilma (ninety-five years of age) does: She calls missionaries and prays for them. I've been on the receiving end of a number of those prayers, and I am grateful for her ministry. She told me she makes so many calls that Chuck got her another phone because he could never get through to her.

I think I have a couple of options going forward. I have worked in many countries where senior adults are respected and revered. When I served in China, the young people would fight over who got to sit by the oldest person in the room. The Chinese consider it an honor to be near someone with a lifetime of wisdom, and they treat the elderly with respect and dignity. The only problem? I don't speak their language.

I have also worked in cultures that make sure elderly people have a way to feel like a productive part of the family. I witnessed this the first time I served among the Wounaan tribe in Panama. The oldest woman in the tribe was bedridden. Each morning, the villagers would pick her up and put her on a mat. Then they dragged her across the compound to the area where they were cooking the evening meal. They placed her next to the fire and gave her a palm leaf. She lay there all day, fanning the fire to keep the coals burning. The men would go hunting, the women would wash clothes, and the children would go off to school, but she kept the fire going until they all came back to cook dinner. After they ate, they would drag her back to her hut for the night. But she was a part of the tribe and had a significant task.

I have also served in the Guna people group. This is another jungle tribe that gives its elderly a position of significance. The first time I visited there, they prepared a welcome meal. We had the usual staples: mashed yucca, tilapia, plantains, rice, and a special treat: creamed corn. I love creamed corn and couldn't believe they had something like this in the jungle. When I told them how much I loved this dish, they piled it on.

At the end of the meal, I thanked them for the delicious food, especially the creamed corn. The villagers told me that two elderly ladies who had no teeth were responsible for creaming the corn. When they noticed the puzzled look on my face, they explained the process. The younger ladies would cook the corn and take it to the older women. After giving the corn a good chewing, these two would spit it back into the bowl as "creamed" corn. I felt a little queasy after that. And I've never eaten another bowl of creamed corn in the jungle again.

But everyone needs significance. My concern about losing it is what I think a lot of us entering this realm of life are facing. After all, we live in a culture that doesn't value the older generation.

But I thank God that my significance comes from Him.

He has called me to be salt and light in this world. And that doesn't stop when you sign up for Medicare. Look at Moses; he started his ministry when he was eighty years old.

So as long as I have two teeth in my head and can engage with those around me, I pray I can be a blessing to someone each day. And when those two teeth are gone, I will just move into the village with the Guna and help cream their corn.

Country Churches, Part 1

I grew up attending small country churches. In fact, when I was growing up, there was no such thing as a megachurch. We didn't have a clue about bands, light shows, or PowerPoint. If you had asked me what a megachurch was, I might have pointed you toward a church in town that had 300 in attendance. It was bigger than my elementary and middle schools combined.

But these small country churches molded my life. Even today, I can't drive by one of those little white wooden structures without remembering how faithful the church members were to teach me the Word of God. I thank God for these rural churches.

As I thought about these small country churches, I realized they have many characteristics in common. In fact, you know you're in a small country church when:

•The pastor, the chairman of the deacons, the music director, and the women's mission leader all have the same last name.

• The church has a board up front announcing how many are in attendance today and how many attended a year ago, and the number is the same. But that might change soon; Uncle Buck's health is not the best.

• The basement/fellowship hall reminds everyone of the empty tomb: dark and damp with a musty smell.

• More people will be caught up in the rapture outside in the cemetery than those who are inside the church.

• The carry-in dinners could qualify for a Michelin five-star rating.

• The members bring their own livestock to use in the Christmas pageant.

The opening of deer season coincides with the annual men's retreat.

- While holding hands in prayer, you notice the women's palms are just as calloused as the men's.

- One family (or the pastor) goes on vacation, and the size of the children's ministry drops by half.

- The bus repair kit includes baling wire.

- The bathroom is in a separate building from the sanctuary.

- Someone's cows are on the prayer list.

Of course, there is no such thing as a small church.

There is only one church, and that is the body of Christ.

We gather together in all kinds of sizes, shapes, and places, and this living organism called the church stretches across the ages.

Your church may do things differently than mine, but that doesn't make one better than the other. Some of you may meet in a sanctuary and others, in an arena. I have preached in churches that gathered under a tree or in a hut, but no matter where the church meets, its job is the same: to evangelize the lost. You see, we exist for those who are outside us.

The church is not a building or a place, but people who have been redeemed and are being trained to use their spiritual gifts to invite others into a relationship with a living, loving God. That's what those small churches I grew up in did. They gave me the skills and knowledge to walk out the life of Christ. And that can happen in a 10,000-seat auditorium or under a tree. Together, we are the church.

One of the other things I remember about our small country church was that during harvest time, you brought part of your crop to share with others. It was not unusual to see people carrying in baskets of potatoes, carrots, and corn. One year, my dad planted popcorn by accident and ended up with somewhere around fifty bushels of the stuff. So what did we do with it? We took it to church and gave everyone a lifetime supply. And the leftovers? We put them at the end of our driveway with a sign that read, "Free Popcorn."

That reminds me of the first church. "All the believers were together and had everything in common. They sold property and possessions to give to anyone who had need" (Acts 2:44-45).

You see? Maybe the small, rural churches aren't so small after all.

Country Churches, Part 2

As I wrote last week, I grew up in small country churches. We didn't have staff members, a digital billboard, or even a paid janitor. We did have janitors, though. Each week, a different family was assigned that duty. When it was your family's turn, your parents would bring you and your siblings to the church to mop, dust, and empty the trash.

I think they now have laws against child labor like this. But we also worked at home and on the farm, so working at the church was normal. And we had to make sure we cleaned as well as the family who did it the week before. We took pride in cleaning our church. I have lots of fond memories of growing up in a church like that.

This week, I want to share ten things I liked about growing up in a small country church:

1. EVERYBODY KNEW EVERYBODY: Each Sunday

was a family reunion. I knew the people in the church better than some of my own relatives. We met on Sunday morning, Sunday night, at someone's house after church on Sunday night, Monday night visitation, Wednesday night prayer meeting, and then again on Sunday.

2. WE CELEBRATED EVERYTHING: From birthdays to anniversaries, from baptisms to graduations to funerals—every event was attended by all. Most of all, we celebrated people. No matter who you were, if something special happened in your life, it was special to us. I remember my Aunt Donna giving me a quarter for being baptized.

If I'd known money was involved, I would probably have been baptized sooner.

---

3. IF YOU WEREN'T THERE, YOU WERE MISSED: Nobody sat in your pew while you were gone. In a small church, we became creatures of habit. Yes, each Sunday, we all sat in the same pew and didn't dare change God's natural order. When a visitor showed up and sat in our seat, we felt like the Holy Spirit had left. We weren't very good at hearing God's Word if we were looking at the preacher from a different angle.

4. I WAS THE YOUTH GROUP: Oh, there might have been one or two other people, but for the most part, everyone was either older or younger than I was. It's difficult to divide up for small group discussion when there are only three of you.

5. WHEN YOU HURT, EVERYONE ELSE HURT: I was nine years old when my mom lost her third child, a little girl, during delivery. This was my first time to experience the pain of death. The church came alongside our family and mourned with us. They held our hands and hearts and walked every step with us during those difficult days.

6. EVERYONE HAD MANY JOBS: Even as a child, I was given the task of handing out bulletins, taking up the offering, cleaning the church, and, on occasion, I even played the piano on Sunday nights. By the time I got to high school, I was a Sunday school teacher. We didn't have enough people to fill every position, so everyone played multiple roles.

7. THE CHURCH WAS CROSS-GENERATIONAL: Even if your grandparents attended the same church, every other senior adult also become your grandparent. Having multiple grandparents speaking our worth and value into us shaped many of our lives. And everyone else? They became our aunts, uncles, and cousins. We were just family.

8. YOUTH CAMPS WERE DIFFERENT: While the big-city churches went to fancy camps, we would go to smaller ones. For us, arts and crafts meant painting the camp director's house, and the tabernacle was more like a sweat lodge. Maybe that is why so many kids got saved. The room was as hot as the place the preacher kept talking about.

9. YOU KNEW WHAT TO WEAR: In those days, you had only three types of clothes—no, make that four. You had your school clothes, your work clothes, your play clothes, and finally, your church clothes. Wearing the wrong clothing at the wrong time was equal to breaking one of the Ten Commandments. The only exception was if you got a new pair of bib overalls, you could wear them to church.

10. CHURCH WAS THE BEST PLACE ON EARTH

There was not a place on earth that was more of a sweet spot for my life than that small country church. We didn't have much, but we had the Bible and a commitment to be the body of Christ to one another.

I may have moved away from that small church and ministered in some of the largest churches in America, but inside, I am still that little boy who longs to find that place again. God bless our small country churches.

Bob Loves You

Greetings from Panama! Our students are spending thirty-five days this summer studying the doctrine of love. They are not only reading what the Bible says about love but putting it into practice with their teammates and the people we serve on the mission field. I don't know much about grammar, but I do know this: Love is a verb.

Love is also important to Jesus. When He was about to return to heaven, He told His disciples, "A new command I give you: Love one another. As I have loved you, so you must love one another. By this everyone will know you are my disciples, if you love one another" (John 13:34-35).

Love is our most distinguishing characteristic as Christ-followers. We love not as the world does but as He has loved us. And there is a huge difference between what is touted as love on television and the internet and what the Bible describes as love. I'm learning alongside the students as we explore true love's many facets.

As I sit here writing this article, my body is covered with chiggers and mosquito bites, and I itch like crazy. I earned these badges of honor in the jungle while the student missionaries and I were telling an indigenous group of people an important truth.

Bob loves them and has a wonderful plan for their lives.

I went even deeper, telling them that Bob loved them so much that He took their place on the cross and died for them. I also gave them the good news that if they repented of their sins, Bob would give them eternal life and take them to live with Him forever.

It may sound funny that we were talking to people about Bob, but in the village where we were working, guess what the word for "God" is? Yep, it's *Bob*. We came thousands of miles to tell the people about Bob.

I have a good friend at the Baptist Messenger named Bob. I admire him a great deal, but he is not God. Lately, I've been thinking a lot about the God Bob. There isn't much else to do here when it gets dark and all the missionaries scramble to get under their nets before the mosquitoes show up in force. It's funny how Bob reveals Himself to me in those moments.

The other night, I was lying in my hammock, looking out through the mosquito netting, when I noticed that the world looks fuzzy when observed from the inside of a net. I've spent many years sleeping under mosquito nets and never thought much about it. But that night, Bob brought it to my attention that the same veil that keeps me safe from the insects makes the outside world look blurry. When I talk to someone through the net, all I can see is that person's outline.

And that's how God looks to the world: a featureless, untouchable identity. That's the way it was for me. I knew there was a God; nature reveals Him. I knew there had to be a mastermind behind all the trees, flowers, sunsets, and other elements all around us. At that point in my life, I had an awareness of God but couldn't see him clearly.

In all the years I've spent going into remote villages, I've never yet found one that didn't know there was a bob. In fact, they've come close to identifying Him. They have sun bobs, moon bobs, and bobs of their crops. They have bobs to help you have children and bobs to help the children find the right spouse. They have bobs of love and bobs of wrath, bobs of peace and bobs of war. Those who worship these bobs are all looking through a veil.

But when the real Bob shows up, He makes everything clear.

Last night was my final night of teaching in the village for several weeks. I told the people I would return soon, but before I left, I had to tell them about Bob one more time. As I gave the invitation, the mosquito nets were lifted. One by one, the people all gave their hearts to Bob.

Each of us has a bob we worship, but maybe yours is hidden behind the veil of a mosquito net. Is something keeping you from seeing the real Bob? First John 4:8 tells us, "Bob is love," so if your Bob is only a hazy image, your understanding of love is almost sure to be hazy, too.

How does the world know Bob has sent us? By our love for one another (John 13:35). Show them the deep, deep love of Bob—today.

Mom's Purse

"Don't leave home without it." This advice applies first, last and always to a mother's purse.

When I was growing up, Mom's purse seemed to hold every object known to mankind. One day, she was driving my brothers and me to the country home of two sisters who sold eggs for a living. Although we were sure they'd gone to nursery school with Moses, these ladies had New Testament names: Mary and Martha. Martha, the youngest and a dead ringer for the queen of England (as long as you squinted your eyes), gave two of us Moore boys piano lessons once a week.

One afternoon, we were barreling down the dirt road for our weekly lessons when our old pickup caught fire. In those days, we four boys rode in the truck bed. When we saw smoke billowing out from underneath the hood and pouring over the roof, we knew we'd hit the jackpot. Few things make little boys more excited than the combination of a good fire and the possibility of skipping piano lessons.

As we peered through the cab window, we could see the tongues of orange and red flickering out from under the hood. My mom, with incredible calm, steered the pickup to the side of the road. Purse draped over her forearm, she got out, strode to the front of the truck, bent over and opened the hood. A puff of smoke rolled forth that, to our young eyes, looked like the cloud that accompanies an atomic blast.

When the smoke cleared, we could see that the carburetor was on fire. Calm as ever, Mom opened her purse and rummaged around inside to produce a wet washrag.

She raised her weapon high and began to flick it at the flames with the accuracy of Zorro's sword.

The more they roared, the more she whipped. The fire must have realized the superiority of its opponent because before long, it fell into submission.

My brothers and I stood in awe, our mouths hanging open. For once, we were speechless. In a few seconds,

Mom had taken that beast from flame to fizzle. With a wet washrag in hand, that woman could tame the devil himself. She turned and, with no change of expression, ordered us back into the pickup bed while she closed the hood. She climbed back inside, revved up the engine, and drove on to piano lessons as though nothing unusual had happened.

Living in rural America as we did, Mom's purse was the closest to an Ace Hardware store any of us had ever seen. From the depths of that pocketbook, she could pull out a dainty hanky to wipe away the tears of a grieving friend or a Phillips-head screwdriver to fix the hinges on a door. But the one thing you could always count on Mom having in her purse was a New Testament. God's Word was important to both my parents. Later in life, my Dad became very involved with the Gideons. He poured time, effort, and funds into making sure others could have Bibles of their own.

Long before that, though, Mom had a passion for putting the Word of God into children.

Every week, she drove that same pickup all over the countryside where we lived. She loved nothing better than to load it up with children, take them to the church, and teach them about the love of Christ. Week after week, she placed cutouts of biblical characters on a flannel board as she explained the truths of Scripture. Salvation came and lives were changed because of Mom's faithful witness.

Mom passed away at an early age on aisle two of the IGA grocery store. The paramedics tried to resuscitate her, but to no avail. A sudden heart attack had taken her life. Only hours before she died, Mom was teaching yet one more group of children, placing some ragged-looking cutouts on a flannel board so she could tell the kids about Jesus.

When the paramedics opened Mom's purse to look for an ID, I can't imagine what they thought. I don't know if they found a wet washrag among the myriad of essentials there, but I know they didn't have to look far to see her New Testament.

My mom's purse reminds of what Jesus wants from us. As we go through life, we ought to keep both the hankies and the hardware close at hand.

But when it comes right down to it, all we really need is the Word of God and a wet washrag. Both come in sizes that make them easy to carry. And both come in handy for putting out fires.

The Big Dipper

My name is Walker Moore, and I am a dipper. My wife says I don't really like food; I only use it as something to dip. I like barbecue sauces, honey mustard sauces, tomato sauces, steak sauces, garlic sauces, sweet and sour sauces… and don't even get me started on the hot sauces.

Since I'm a missionary, my taste also extends to the likes of Asian sauces, German sauces, Chinese sauces, Caribbean Satay sauces, Brazilian sauces, Chilean lime sauces, and Hungarian paprika sauces.

There has not been a country to whose sauces God has not called me.

I dip my chicken, my French fries, my tortilla chips, and my bread. In fact, there is no food I can think of that I won't dip into some kind of sauce. Of course, there are those purists who believe you shouldn't put anything on a steak: no A.1. Sauce, no Heinz 57 Sauce, and the cardinal rule: No ketchup should ever touch a steak. The meat juices are the only sauce you need.

I was visiting the Florida home of my pastor friend Nathan Blackwell and his lovely wife Trish one evening when he cooked a delicious barbecue steak dinner. Like me, he thinks a steak can taste delicious in its own juices but also enjoys manipulating the taste to make it completely different. That night, he used a unique mustard barbeque sauce. I bit into that steak, and my taste buds burst with flavor as though they were participating in a Fourth of July fireworks display.

When I returned home, I bragged and bragged about this delicious sauce, telling my wife and staff all about it. I had never tasted anything like it. I came home from work the other day, and there on our front porch sat a white USPS box. Inside lay two sixteen-ounce bottles of Jimmy Bear's Original BBQ sauce, a gift from my dear friends.

That reminds me: Did you know Jesus was a Baptist? Our denomination has a well-known propensity for fellowship meals where we mix great theology with some of the world's best carry-in dinners. Why else do you think I'm a Baptist?

Jesus' life bears this out. Some of His greatest miracles had to do with food. Remember when He turned water into wine? The wine He made was the best of the evening and became the topic of conversation late into the night. And remember how Peter was out trying to catch some food? His nets remained empty, so Jesus told him to cast them out on the other side of the boat. Peter obeyed, and his nets came up so full they nearly burst.

All four Gospels record the feeding of the five thousand. The disciples had no way to feed the masses, so Jesus took a little boy's five loaves and two fish, blessed them, and distributed them. The crowd ate until everyone was satisfied, and the leftovers totaled twelve heaping baskets full.

Another time, Jesus fed a crowd of four thousand who had been hanging out listening to Him for three days. You can bet that when the people got home, they told story after story about the amazing things Jesus did with food.

I believe God designed us as creatures who are intended to dine together. A unique interaction takes place over meals that can only happen at the table among family and friends.

Yet somehow in our busy lives, we have forsaken the family meal.

I suggest that you turn off the TV, call your entire family to the dinner table, and engage in the old-time art of conversation. By this I mean not, "How was your day?" but "What do you think about what's happening in Venezuela?" or "Can you remember last Sunday's sermon? What point was our pastor trying to make?" Mealtime can be a great place to place a godly foundation in a child's life as you teach listening and thinking skills along the way.

As I write this article, I am in the country of Panama, trying to teach students to be like Jesus. Do you know the first two characteristics Scripture reveals about Him? Luke 2:46 tells us His parents found Him in the temple courts with the teachers, "listening to them and asking them questions."

These two characteristics served Jesus well for the rest of His life. He listened to the woman at the well and the solider whose servant was sick. He also asked tremendous questions.

In fact, asking questions was one of the main ways He taught others. Ask God to show you ways to use your family mealtimes to help your child develop these Christ-like qualities.

Now, would someone please pass the barbecue sauce?

Make Your Kids Take Shop

This past weekend, I visited my oldest son, Jeremiah, and daughter-in-love Erin in Rockwall, Texas. They have recently moved there and are both teaching school.

Upon arrival, I was greeted by the normal hugs and exchanges of affection—along with a broken vacuum sweeper. They were trying to install a new belt but didn't have any instructions.

Always the dad, I set about to solve my children's problems. It finally took all three of us to accomplish the task: one to pry open the plastic case, one to slip the belt inside, and the third to stretch it around the beater brush. The next day, I had so much fun being with my children: fixing their computer, running wires through the walls and, once again, being a dad.

I confess to you that, for a long time, I considered myself a failure when it came to my children's education.

It was always embarrassing for me, a grown man, to confess to the world that I had permanently damaged my boys.

You see, I woke up one day and realized a horrible truth: My sons never took shop.

When Jeremiah and Caleb were young, we enrolled them in magnet schools. Supposedly, this would give them an advantage when it came time for college. At these magnet schools, they received the most up-to-date, innovative teaching, designed to equip them for Harvard and beyond. Cathy and I thought we were being good parents, but both our boys made it through high school without taking even one shop course. I understand most high schools still offer shop, but I never hear about anyone actually taking it.

In my high school, every young man took either shop or auto mechanics. I loved shop! It is the best memory from my five years of high school. While my classmates were turning out walnut ashtrays and salad bowls, I made my parents a solid maple, seven-drawer dresser (no, I am not making this up).

Today's students take more unusual, intellectual classes. Jeremiah took meteorology. He can describe a dozen different cloud formations and waxes eloquent on the subject of barometric pressure. Caleb, on the other hand, took photography. One son could tell you when it is going to rain; the other could take pictures of the rain; but neither one could fix the roof. They did not learn how to use a hammer—so what good was all that information?

For the longest time, my boys' diplomas sat on their desks. Neither one knew how to drive in a nail to hang the thing up. Oh, they knew how to wire up a Nintendo game or splice the cable TV from one bedroom to the other. They could hook up the multiple wires on back of their computer; connect the mouse, the modem, the monitor, the scanner, the keyboard, and a host of other paraphernalia, but even changing a burned-out light bulb extended past their range of handyman ability.

After my sons were grown, all I heard from them at first were things like, "Dad, our faucet is dripping." "Dad, the toilet is stopped up." Somewhere in all those years of education, someone should have taught them how to use a plunger. And somehow during their years in high school, someone should teach students that when the red light on the dash comes on, it doesn't mean you've got a week to figure out what's wrong. Take my advice: Make your kids take shop.

Educating your children encompasses two areas: knowledge and skills.

Knowledge is the easy part, but giving your children skills takes patience, practice, and mentoring. If I could do life over again, I would spend more time helping my children learn the skills of living. Working on small projects helps prepare them for the bigger ones life sends their way.

By now, both my sons have picked up some skills from their dad. Jeremiah has now built an armoire for his TV; he refers to it as the "masterpiece." Caleb has recently retiled his bathroom. But there are other areas of their lives— especially spiritual things—that I could have mentored more effectively.

I like to tell parents, "You pay now, or you pay later." Teach your children how to pray, how to search the Scriptures and give an answer for what they believe. Knowledge is good, but knowledge empowered with skills is freedom.

Dear Father, help me to impart to my children the tools of knowledge, then teach them the skills to use these tools effectively. May the knowledge they grasp become as a scalpel in a practiced surgeon's hands. Thank You for giving me the skills I need to be an effective parent today. Amen.

To the Little Girl in the Yellow Dress

Dear Little Girl in the Yellow Dress,

Not long ago, you and I sat on a plane together. You tried to show me how old you were, but you had trouble keeping all four fingers up at the same time. Like all children your age, you were wide-eyed and cute as a newborn kitten.

You were at the perfect age to share everything you knew with anyone who would listen. You told me your name, your dogs' names, and your doll's name. You told me about your baby brother and how he cries all the time. And then you showed me how you cover your ears when he gets too loud.

I watched you squint your eyes and put your hands over your mouth as you giggled.

You asked if I had any kids, and I told you I had two boys. You weren't impressed.

You asked if I had a dog, and I told you I used to, but she got old and died. You gave me a sad look and then started singing and brushing your doll's hair. What a wonderful age you are!

As I sat beside your sweet innocence, I felt an overwhelming urge to pray for you. You see, I know things about this world that you don't yet know. As you chattered away, I asked God to place a hedge of protection around you. In the future, wolves dressed in sheep's clothing will appear at your doorstep. They'll tell you anything to satisfy their carnal hunger and then leave as fast as they came. And sometimes, these wolves won't even bother putting on sheep's clothing. They'll come, take whatever they want, and leave you in broken pieces. Unless God does a work in your life, you'll spend the rest of your days trying to put it back together. My dear little girl in the yellow dress, I pray this will never happen to you.

There's so much I wish I could talk to you about. I'd like to encourage you to find a godly woman who is wise to the ways of the world but wiser to the things of God. Choose someone who will walk beside you and mentor you about how to become a Proverbs 31 woman. She'll teach you how to discern a good and godly man, someone who will do everything in his power to guard your innocence.

Little girl in the yellow dress, you don't know this, but I've spent almost forty years of my life trying to teach little boys how to become men. I didn't do very well in the beginning, but as I've grown, I've redoubled my efforts. I do my best to cast the truth in to these young boys and call it out of them as they step into their manhood. Growing up, I learned a lot about the Bible, but no one ever taught me how to walk as a good and godly man. When I tried to figure it out, I struggled and failed.

Today, I take my rightful place. We have only an hour and fifteen minutes together, but as the closest man to you right now, I'm asking the Creator to bring men into your life who reflect Him.

As I sit beside you, I know you are "fearfully and wonderfully made" (Ps. 139:14).

I didn't make this up; it's written in God's holy book.
The enemy wants to take away from you three things:
your worth, your beauty, and your innocence. I pray that
one day, you'll find a man who reflects what our heavenly
Father says about each one of these.

I've seen many young men like this step into their
roles, and that's good. When you look for a man, you don't
need a Savior, because we already have one. His name is
Jesus. But you do need a man who walks in sync with his
Creator. I pray that one day, you'll find one of the men I've
discipled. He'll know how to speak your worth and value
into you. He'll proclaim your beauty to the world and
know how to reflect the heavenly Father through a touch.
Yes, little girl in the yellow dress, there are men like that
out there. Please don't settle for anyone less.

Well, the plane is about ready to land, and our paths
may never cross again. But today, I thought of you and
prayed that my God in heaven would answer my prayers
on your behalf.

When you grow up, I pray you'll find the man He has
for you, the kind who will one day pray for the one who sits
next to him on the airplane: the little girl in the yellow dress.

Your servant, Walker Moore

I Can't Spel

You would think since I've written a book and have a weekly column that I must have a degree in English or writing, but I don't. I went to a conservative Christian college and received a Bachelor of Science in Liberal Studies. That means I took lots of classes but didn't major in anything.

I must confess something: I can't spel.

Growing up, I wasn't the sharpest crayon in the box.

Because I didn't speak very clearly, everyone assumed I would spend most of my life in the bottom half of the class. I don't feel too bad about that. Albert Einstein's parents considered him a slow child, and I've read that he didn't speak very well until he was nine years old. When his parents asked his teachers what profession they should guide him toward, the teachers said it didn't matter; he would be a failure no matter what. I like to think neither Albert nor I was slow; we were just late bloomers.

One of the most difficult subjects for me was spelling. Every week, we had the dreaded spelling test. And our little country school had ways of motivating young students. If you made a hundred percent on your spelling test, you got a free ticket to the Saturday matinee. To a young boy in rural America, going to the theater was a mystical, magical experience. I worked hard trying to learn to spell those words, only to get seventy-five or eighty out of one hundred on my paper.

Unlike Albert, who said he couldn't remember much of his childhood, I do remember mine; I just choose not to recall everything. It wasn't my fault I couldn't spell. The blame goes to whoever invented the English language. Take the word psychology. There is no reason on earth for it to start with a "p." And if it starts with a "p," then you should pronounce that letter: "p-ssssyychoolooogy." It even sounds better when you sound out all the letters. I can think of only one reason to throw in extra letters in a word, and that's to keep a third-grade boy from getting 100 on his spelling test.

One day, I was sitting in class, and the teacher was passing out our graded spelling tests. She handed over mine with a big smile, for on top of the paper was written a bright red 100. And attached to it was a ticket to the matinee showing of *Gulliver's Travels*.

Even though I wasn't a speller, I was a reader, and I had read Jonathan Swift's famous novel. That next Saturday, as the lights dimmed, I was drawn into Lemuel Gulliver's travels as he encountered the strange Lilliputians. His journey took him to exotic places like Brobdingnag, Laputa, and even the country of the Houyhnhnms. For the next hour, I was intrigued by each place Gulliver landed.

Looking back, I can see God had already put a yearning for the world in my heart. As I've served Him in many different part of the world, I'm often asked, "What's your favorite country?" My answer is always the same: the last one I served in. That heartbeat for the world in a third-grade boy was given by God and confirmed through books, movies, and especially the Bible.

Even to this day, I'm a terrible speller. The only reason you don't know it is that I have Spel Check on my computer. I wasn't designed to win the school spelling bee, but I was designed by the Creator to engage other cultures. While you're reading this, I'm living in the jungle, sleeping in a hammock under a thatched roof, fighting off mosquitoes, and teaching the Bible in an Embera Wounan village. I have a better job than Gulliver ever did.

Mom and Dad, your child is created for something special. You might have a child like Albert who ends up writing the theory of relativity, or you might have a child who is a poor speller and ends up writing books and living in the jungle.

<hr />

It's never too late to pray for your children to discover what God has for them.

<hr />

Encourage them to dream aloud about their potential.

If God can take a boy like me and make him a writer and an expert at living in remote villages, there's nothing He can't do with your children.

Even if they can't spel.

Cheap Airfare

How often do you hear someone complain about a recent plane flight? The entire airline industry is experiencing some difficulties. As a frequent flyer, I always look for the cheapest way to get from Point A to Point B. You can tell you're using a cheap airline when:

• They don't use "tickets" but refer to them as "chances" instead.

• All the insurance machines in the terminal are sold out.

• Before the flight, the passengers get together to elect a pilot.

• You can't board the plane unless you have exact change.

• The captain asks all the passengers to chip in to help pay for gas.

You ask the captain how often planes crash, and he says, "Just once."

• You don't need a movie on the flight because your life keeps flashing before your eyes.

• The airline's slogan is "We're Amtrak—with Wings," or the company advertises, "Your kids will love our slides."

• And finally, you know you're on a cheap airline when all the planes have a bathroom and a chapel.

A few years ago, I was boarding a plane to Dothan, Alabama, when the flight attendants announced it was experiencing mechanical difficulties, and we would need to change equipment. (They should just say, "Folks, this plane is broken. We'll have to move you to another plane and hope it will fly.")

Out came the next piece of "equipment": a tiny prop plane to replace the brand-new jet we had just boarded. This plane looked as though it been pulled from a museum and hadn't flown in years. It had a flat tire, and the only thing that seemed to be holding it together was its spotty, rust-streaked coat of paint. However, I was relieved to hear the flight attendant say we'd be on our way as soon as they aired up the flat.

With the airplane loaded and the doors closed, the flight attendant began to go through the safety procedures—until the pilot paged her. This tiny plane was overloaded, so someone would have to switch flights. Who would volunteer?

A long period of silence usually follows this type of question. But this time, the flight attendant had hardly finished her sentence when a man volunteered. He must have raised his hand faster than the rest of us who wanted to get off that rust bucket with wings. Our one lucky volunteer left.

Again, the door closed, and the flight attendant began her spiel when we heard "Urrrrrrh, urrrrh, urrrh, urh." This time, the engine wouldn't start.

The door opened once more to allow a mechanic to board. For forty minutes, all we heard was the "Urrrrh, urrrh, urh" sound. At one point, the mechanic yelled, "I think I got the backup batteries working." Now, the last thing I want to hear from an airplane mechanic is the phrase, "I think." I want him to know whatever was wrong is now fixed and the plane is fit to fly.

Finally, the plane took off, and I spent the entire flight in prayer. Sometimes a bargain ticket comes at a high price. The moral of this story? You get what you pay for. And the same rule often applies to parenting.

Your parenting shouldn't be accidental, but intentional.

God's Word speaks to this type of intentionality: "These are the commands, decrees, and laws the LORD your God directed me to teach you to observe in the land that you are crossing the Jordan to possess, so that you, your children and their children after them may fear the LORD your God as long as you live by keeping all his decrees and commands that I give you, and so that you may enjoy long life" (Deut. 6:1-2).

God wants us to teach and lead our children to be "doers of the word and not merely hearers who delude themselves" (James 1:22, NASB). Mom and Dad, it isn't enough to give your children head knowledge. They need to have the skills to handle choices and challenges in and through His holy Word. Their lives depend on it.

Ephesians 6:1-3 says the same thing. If children learn to submit their lives to the Word of God, they will live long and well. Isn't that what you want for your children?

In this season of new life, resolve to become a parent who brings life to the children under your care, one who not only teaches them to know God's Word but to have a heartbeat of obedience.

After all, you don't want your plane—or your parenting—to crash.

Audience of One

There are two principles I try to instill into every student who sits under our ministry. They are not easy principles to teach, and I can't share them on demand, but only by the timing of the Lord.

As most of you know, I am first and foremost a missionary for the Lord Jesus Christ. I organize students to go around the world, evangelize the lost, and plant churches, while at the same time equipping them to walk as men and women of God.

Our ministry isn't like most missions organizations. We believe before students go on the mission field, they must lay down their adolescences and pick up their adult responsibilities. We evaluate how "adult" they are by using 1 Timothy 4:12, where the apostle Paul gives young Timothy five characteristics of adulthood. He lists the five as speech, conduct, love, faith (faithfulness), and purity. If you violate any one of these five, people will not take you seriously as an emerging adult. The bottom line: I can't take "teenagers" to the mission field because the messenger always gets in the way of the message.

Their childish behavior hinders their effectiveness in sharing the gospel message.

As I teach about true adulthood, I also instill a principle I call the "Audience of One." It says that no matter what it is, ultimately, every job or task is done "unto the Lord" (1 Cor. 10:31). The only audience that really matters is Jesus Christ.

Another principle is the flip side of Audience of One, and I call this one "The Keeper." When David went off to the battle, he left his sheep with the keepers. Keepers have the ability to do a job without receiving any recognition or accolades; they are satisfied with the knowledge that the only one who knows what they are doing is the Lord, and His recognition is enough. When these two principles come together in a believer's life, they bring an intense peace about what you are doing. You know who you are working for, and you know that it only matters what He thinks of your service.

The other day, both principles again came home in my life. I was preaching in the jungles of Panama to a group of new believers. We were celebrating the third anniversary of their church. The first year our ministry was there, it was a home church; our second year, it became a mission; and this year, it is a full-fledged church and has already started a Bible study in the next village down the road. Thursday night, we walked to the church in a torrential rain to sit under a tin roof held up by eight poles over a dirt floor and a few crude homemade benches for us to sit on. That night, our team presented the gospel in drama, sang some songs, and then my youngest son, Caleb, brought the message.

As we were singing, we noticed a little lady standing out in the downpour. One of our team members motioned for her to come in and sit down. She was wearing clothes that you knew someone had given her because the sleeves had been cut off and the threads were unraveling.

At the end of the service, the pastor announced that we had a special guest. I thought, *I am special, and I am a guest* when he announced, "Sister Sehunda is with us tonight."

I didn't know who Sister Sehunda was, but the pastor told us that it had taken her sixteen hours to walk the eighteen miles across the mountain. She had left at three-thirty in the morning to hike across steep, rugged terrain to come and encourage the new believers in the church. He asked her to stand, and the little old lady we had invited in out of the rain stood up. The pastor asked if she had a song in her heart.

"I had a glorious day of praising God as I walked the sixteen hours in the rain. I think I might have one more song in my heart," she said with a twinkle in her eyes. This little lady, who couldn't have been any more than four feet tall, raised one hand, the strings dangling from her sleeves, and began to sway as she sang in her native tongue. I will swear upon a stack of Bibles that the entire jungle started swaying with her, and it was very evident she was singing not to us but unto the Lord.

When she finished, a holy hush fell over the room. Not a word was said, not a muscle moved.

We had just witnessed a Keeper singing for an Audience of One.

I had the chance to visit with her afterward, and she said she was going to get a few hours' sleep and make the sixteen-hour trek back home the next day.

Sister Sehunda doesn't know she is being written about and would be embarrassed if she knew I had lifted her up as an example. She knows who she did it for, and that's all that counts. I fell on my face after the service that night, asking God to forgive me for being self-centered and not Savior-centered. Maybe the reason our children haven't learned these principles is because we parents haven't learned them ourselves.

By the way, did I tell you Sister Sehunda is seventy years old, has a heart condition, and has only been saved for seven years herself? But she understands about being a Keeper for an Audience of One.

The Great Hymnal Robbery

In the late fifties, our little country church congregation was split down the middle. The older people wanted to keep the hymnals we already had, but the younger generations wanted a new hymnal that contained some of the more contemporary hymns.

Now, if you know anything about Baptists, you know they are the most agreeable and gracious people on earth—until they don't get their way.

We held a well-attended business meeting where both old and young presented their sides. The older people shared their love for the tried-and-true hymns. These classics contained sound doctrine, they explained, and people visiting from other churches would feel out of place with new-fangled hymnals.

Then the younger people presented their side. Music had changed over the years, they said, and they wanted hymns that would attract their generation. They preferred the new hymnal that contained both old and new hymns. But the frugal older congregation had come out of the Great Depression and didn't think it would be wise to spend so much money on new hymnals.

This argument went on for months—until one day, someone broke into the church and stole the hymnals right out of the pews.

The younger church members weren't too upset about the robbery, but the older ones walked around, stunned. The police were called in, and even the local newspaper reported on "The Great Hymnal Robbery."

The police questioned many of the younger folks. They concluded that either the younger members of the congregations were good at protecting the thief or they really didn't know anything about who might have done it. To this day, the perpetrator has never been caught, and no one has come forward to confess. I was disappointed not to be interrogated or fingerprinted. I guess a seven-year boy wasn't considered a likely suspect.

In our county, stealing a hymnal was almost as serious as stealing someone's dog. There was a lot of speculation about who did it and why.

Back then, a Baptist church without hymnals was like a guitar without strings.

Our church called an emergency business meeting, and the new hymnals were approved. Months went by, and we adjusted to the change. The music leader made sure those on each side of the dispute had several of their favorites sung each Sunday. So instead of one side being totally disappointed over the song selection every week, both sides were only half disappointed.

Fall turned to winter and winter to spring. Our little church held its annual revival with great success, as several of the people we were praying for in our community came to saving grace that week.

In our church, a baptismal service ranked right up there next to a potluck dinner. But our little church didn't have one of those modern-day baptistries. Instead, the floor of the platform was the door of the baptistry. Someone would come in on Saturday and raise the floor to reveal a concrete vault that looked like one used in a cemetery to hold a coffin. In fact, to a young boy with a vivid imagination who observed these baptisms, the words "buried with Christ" took on a dual meaning. But on this particular Saturday, when the floor was raised before filling the vault with water, there in the bottom of the baptistry lay the missing hymnals. They hadn't been stolen after all.

When the older members heard of this great discovery, you would have thought the ark of the covenant had been found. The next day, when the members gathered to worship, they had their choice of hymnals from which to sing "Amazing Grace," and everyone went home happy.

Yes, this is a true story. As one who has spent over forty years ministering in churches, I have seen church members argue about so many things: coffee, carpet, colors, and everything in between.

> ## Looking back, I know those arguments didn't add to the growth of the kingdom.

They were just ploys of the enemy to sidetrack us from the main things. When we are busy studying His Word, praying for the lost, and meeting the needs of the hurting in our church and community, we don't really have much time to argue over things like hymnals.

Whatever happened to those hymnals, anyway? Most churches don't use them anymore. If you're going to have an argument, argue over things of eternal value; that is what really matters. Maybe that's why the wise apostle Paul gave the following advice to young Timothy. "Don't have anything to do with foolish and stupid arguments, because you know they produce quarrels. And the Lord's servant must not be quarrelsome but must be kind to everyone. . ." (2 Tim. 2:23-24).

Luggage Adventures

Recently, my wife and I took a much-needed vacation. It was a short one, just five days, but we loved the rest and the time away. Flying back into Tulsa, we were excited, because we knew Titus the Honorable and Cohen the Goodhearted would be there to greet us. Nothing says "Welcome home" like two little boys yelling your name as soon as they see you.

As we came out of airport security, Titus spotted me and yelled, "Poppy!" Then he ran to give Grammy a big hug. Smart kid. While we were waiting for our luggage to arrive, I pointed to our carry-on suitcase and whispered, "I have a surprise for you."

"What is it, Poppy?"

"I can't tell you; you'll have to wait until we get home."

He kept staring at the suitcase, which I thought was a little weird. When we got home, we opened the suitcase and gave the two boys their presents.

Titus was about excited as someone who had just received a letter from the IRS.

He mumbled, "Thank you" and walked off.

My wife, who is much more perceptive than I am, pulled me to the side and said, "He thought the suitcase was his present."

Now why would a kid who has just turned four years old want a suitcase? I found out that he and his family are planning a short vacation to Branson, Missouri. They plan to stay at a hotel that has a water park inside. In fact, Titus thinks every hotel has a water park inside. While his family was getting ready, he informed them that he needed his own suitcase for his clothes and toys. He has his own backpack, his own sleeping bag, and his own water bottle, so why wouldn't he come to the logical conclusion that he needed his own suitcase?

Later that day, we got a call from his mom, asking if they could borrow one small suitcase. Of course, Grammy being Grammy (she has the spirit of compassion and is the only one who knows the password for our checking account), she suggested we buy one instead.

So Grammy took off on a mission. Watch out, Navy SEALs and Army Rangers. When Grammy goes on a mission, nothing gets in her way. Several hours later, she returned with a child-sized, blue camouflage suitcase.

When Titus entered the house, he spotted it right away. "Whose is this, Grammy?" he asked with a big grin. He knew the answer before she responded.

"It's yours. Grammy got it for you."

"For me?"

"Yes, for you."

Maybe you know the old saying, "A young boy and his suitcase will never part." Well, maybe it isn't that old a saying, but for the rest of the evening, Titus the Honorable dragged that thing all over the house. Up the stairs, down the stairs, "bumpety-bump" we heard as the wheels clattered against the steps. I had to sit down and listen to his lecture on the purpose of each pocket and watch his demonstration on the intricate workings of the zipper. Then he began to dream about the adventures he and his suitcase would have.

"Poppy, when I come back over, I will bring my suitcase, and you and me can go hiking. When we catch a snake, we can put it in my suitcase."

Then it dawned upon me.

It wasn't about the suitcase; it was about the adventure.

It was about preparing for the adventure, going on the adventure, and using the suitcase to hold anything we caught on our adventure. In his little mind, that suitcase opened a whole new world.

And I dreamed right along with him. You see, I carry mountain-climbing carabiners on my backpack. I don't travel without them. I have used them to thread through my belt loops when my belt broke. I have used them to hang my water bottle from the seat in front of me in an airplane. There's always another reason you need a carabiner. I looked at the miniature suitcase. "Titus, you're missing something."

"What's that, Poppy?"

I reached over to my backpack, unhooked one of my carabiners, and snapped it onto his suitcase. The look on his face was priceless. "Poppy, now I have everything I need to go on an adventure."

Yes, young Titus the Honorable, you can look at life one of two ways. Jesus taught me this. You can see the fields, or you can see the fields white unto harvest. "Don't you have a saying, 'It's still four months until harvest'? I tell you, open your eyes and look at the fields! They are ripe for harvest" (John 4:35).

When you see life through Jesus's eyes, it's always an adventure. And you'll need a suitcase every time.

Oil of Olé

It happened in either fifth or sixth grade; I don't remember exactly. For Parents' Night, our class was asked to perform a Mexican dance. Each child was assigned a certain part according to his grace and agility—and I had earned the best one of all. For weeks, I excitedly told my parents all about our rehearsals and my hard work. I wanted to make sure they would both attend my world premiere.

The moment came. My fellow dancers and I waited behind the closed curtains, which soon inched apart, revealing an audience of proud parents. I stood on the back row: hand expertly placed on one hip, head held high, grin spread from ear to ear. As the music began, the children in front of me moved forward. Boys and girls intertwined to dance in a circle, gracefully swirling and bowing. I held my position, watching. My parents' eyes remained glued to their son, waiting for his special part.

Finally, the music wound down. The other children returned. This was my cue. I walked between them, got down on one knee, threw my arms wide, and yelled, "Olé!"

The curtains closed as I held my dramatic position. I hurried from the stage, eager to see my parents' pride in their son's fine performance.

Maybe I wouldn't win an Oscar, but I at least deserved a nomination.

As I ran up to them, I sensed that they had been laughing a little—OK, a lot. Dad kept throwing up his hands and yelling, "Olé, olé!"

"We thought you were in the dance!" they chuckled. All the way home, they kept laughing and repeating, "Olé!"

I never again attempted a school dance.

As an adult, I can see why Mom and Dad thought this was funny. They had waited for my special part in the dance, only to have it consist of a single "Olé!" To me, however, dancing wasn't nearly as important as appearing on stage and having the only speaking part, especially one that involved a foreign language. What was a Mexican dance without a final "Olé"? My parents saw it differently—they thought I wasn't good enough to dance. My stunning performance was relegated to the joke of the year. Even to this day, when I think about it, it still hurts.

I know Mom and Dad didn't mean to cause me pain. And that's my point.

Many parents thoughtlessly say or do things that hurt their children. A child works hard to draw a picture, only to have a parent say, "What in the world is that?" Next time, he doesn't even want to take the crayons out of the box, because he doesn't want to experience more pain.

Would you do me a favor? The next time your child comes home and tells you he got the best part in the school musical, just agree. Many dreams have been dashed by a careless laugh. Olé?

Just Thinking

I had a thought today. I know this surprises you as much as it did me. For the most part, we are not a thinking people. Someone says, "Buy this," and we buy it. Our society has lost the art of thinking. Since we don't think much anymore, we now have people whose job it is to make labels for non-thinkers.

The other day, I saw one of these labels on an iron-on transfer kit to make your own T-shirt design. The label read,

"Do not iron while wearing shirt."

Wouldn't the average person know how dangerous it would be to run an iron across a heat transfer design while wearing the shirt? I guess not.

And then there's the label on the back of a bottle of

children's cough syrups that reads, "Do not drive car or operate heavy machinery." I don't think children should be driving or operating heavy machinery whether they are taking cough syrup or not. But someone wasn't thinking.

The Bible talks a lot about the art of discernment, another term for thinking. In the process of thinking you gather, explore, evaluate, and then assign values to ideas, situations, circumstances, and decisions. Scripture defines two types of thinking: that of a child and that of an adult. "When I was a child, I talked like a child, I thought like a child, I reasoned like a child. When I became a man, I put the ways of childhood behind me" (1 Cor. 13:11).

What's the difference between childish thinking and adult thinking? A true adult uses the Word of God as a part of his thinking process and makes decisions in agreement with God's Word. So do you need a Bible to see if you should iron a decal on your shirt while wearing it? It wouldn't hurt, but it shouldn't be necessary, either.

I love the part in the Bible where Jesus asked His disciples two questions. The first was a non-thinking one, and the other was tremendously deep-thinking. In Mark 8:27, Jesus asked, "Who do people say I am?" His followers didn't have to use even one brain cell to repeat what they had heard. And the answers were easy: "Some say John the Baptist; others say Elijah; and still others, one of the prophets" (Mark 8:28). But Jesus, the master of making people think, turned the question around: "But who do you say I am?" (Mark 8:29). Now that's a question you have to think about. And the answer requires a lot of thinking, too.

Too often, our churches train our children and students to know the answer to the question "Who do other people say I am?" They can quote back what their Sunday school teacher, youth pastor, or senior pastor says, but when the question comes around to "Who do you say I am?" this generation falls apart. They can't give a reasonable defense for the faith.

I've spent my life taking students into cross-cultural situations where Sunday-school answers won't work. Now don't get me wrong. I am a big proponent of Sunday school, but our teaching must move from thinking as a child to theology and apologetics. These subjects equip us for the adult skill of speaking in defense of our faith.

> If we don't teach our children critical thinking, we are raising up the church of Homer Simpson.

I don't know if you have ever seen the television show The Simpsons, and I honestly hope you haven't. But when Homer, the father of the family is put in a situation where he doesn't know the answer or what to do, he says, "D'oh!"

I fear our non-thinking culture is teaching the members of the church, when asked a serious question, to respond by saying, "D'oh!"

"How do you know that Jesus is the Son of God?"

"D'oh!"

"How do you know the Bible is true?"

"D'oh!"

"Is there such a thing as absolute truth?"

"D'oh!"

"How do you know Jesus arose from the grave?"

"D'oh!"

There's a difference between knowing what you believe and understanding why you believe it. Too often, I have seen the church send her students off to college where their faith is questioned.

And too often, they stand there without a reasonable answer. If your faith is shaken and you don't have an answer, it won't be too long before you leave it behind. Your faith is only as good as your ability to defend it.

"Do not deceive yourselves. If any of you think you are wise by the standards of this age, you should become 'fools' so that you may become wise" (1 Cor. 3:18).

Lord, may we be fools to the world and wise in the things of You.

Txt MsgN

My name is Walker Moore, and I don't know how to text message. There, I finally said it. A man who has spent most of his life working with young people can't text. Our students tell me that if I want to communicate with this generation, I need to catch up—and fast.

This sounds fine, except that I have only recently learned to use my computer with its full-size keyboard. Now they want me to stare at my cell phone's miniature keypad and try to type something coherent? I don't know whether you have ever watched students as they text, but it is a sight to behold. Using one hand, they hold their tiny phones. Next, using only one thumb, they pound the tiny little keys until they have tiny little messages on those tiny little screens. Of course, they complete all this in mere seconds.

This generation must have its biggest muscles in the thumbs used for texting.

When you text message, not only do you have to learn to make letters mysteriously appear on your cell phone screen, but you have to learn a whole new language called "text lingo." For example, you might get a text that reads, "Gudam wycm 2moro wif ur adr? HAND!" Translated into normal English, this means, "Good morning. Will you call me tomorrow with your address? Have a nice day!" After spending years learning to spell, the last thing this dyslexic writer wants to hear is that I must learn again.

Text lingo, like other modern forms of teen communication, includes special abbreviations. "BRB" means "Be right back." "LOL" is "laughing out loud" and "gr8" is "great." Some of you parents need to know that "PAL" is "parents are listening" and "PAW" is "parents are watching." In fact, this generation has created its own dictionary so it can text message more rapidly than ever. IDGI. Excuse me; I was practicing my text messaging: "I don't get it."

Not long ago, I talked to a student who told me he got as many as five hundred texts a day. Yet, when I call him, he won't answer his phone. It seems the cell phone has become a text messaging machine instead of an instrument for talking and listening.

Text-impaired people like me can find help in the form of a website (transl8it.com) that allows you to type your message in plain English. It translates your words into "text lingo" with the click of a mouse. Just for fun, I typed in John 3:16 and it came out: "4 God so luvd d wrld dat he gave Hs 1 & onlE Son, dat whoever BlEvz n him shaL not perish bt hav eternal Lyf."

Next, I tried Genesis 1:1, 2: "n d beginN God creatD d heavNz & d erth. nw d erth wz formless & drknez wz Ovr d surfAc of d dEp, & d Spirit of God wz hovRN Ovr d H2Oz. & God sed, 'lt ther b lite,' & ther wz lite.'"

Why has text messaging become so popular? I believe today's young people use it to validate their existence. A part of the ancient path (Jer. 6:16) God has instilled deep within us says we must belong to something bigger than ourselves.

> We need to know we have significance in the lives of others, that we matter.

God planned the family—a place where we could discover our self-worth and validate our existence—to meet this deep need.

That has changed, however, with the shift in our culture. Especially since the sixties, we have been out searching for ourselves. Each generation has sought its own way.

My generation tried sit-ins, love-ins, Woodstock, and finding ourselves in drugs. This generation is trying to validate its existence through technological means including Facebook (yes, you can become my friend on Facebook), Instagram, and text messaging.

Mom, Dad, and grandparents: This generation is crying out for someone to speak into them their worth. They want to hear not merely that they are special but that they are special "because. . . " (you fill in the blank). Look your children or grandchildren in the eye, use their names and then validate them by saying, "I love you because. . . " or, "I appreciate you because. . ." The words that come after "because" validate their existence and give them self-worth.

If you find yourself unable to validate your child or grandchild in this way, maybe you can start by texting. I aPrec8 U Baptist msgR readers cuz I dun hav 2 txt msg my wrds 2 U.

25 Lessons from Camping

I have so many childhood memories of summer vacations. My family was poor. We may not have had enough money to put curtains on our windows, but we did have enough to buy a canvas tent. Every summer, you could count on the fact that the Moores would go camping somewhere. And that "somewhere" usually took us to the mountains of Colorado, Montana, or Wyoming.

My dad had us so organized that when he hit the brakes, we jumped out of the car and set up camp with military precision. My brother Gary and I had the job of putting up the family tent.

We prided ourselves on having it fully functional in three minutes.

Of course, we had some great motivation: sleet, rain, snow, bears, and Dad's rule that no one could go to the bathroom until the tent was set up.

Looking back on those experiences, I want to share some of the lifelong lessons camping has taught me.

1. The shape of a mummy sleeping bag has nothing to do with the human body.

2. No matter which side of the tent you sleep on, yours will be the side that leaks when it rains.

3. There is no such thing as a level campsite. That's a rumor campgrounds use in their brochures.

4. No matter how well you try to clear the debris from the ground under the tent, you'll always find a rock under your sleeping bag.

5. There is no way to keep dirt out of a tent. One day of camping, and you could grow a garden with the amount of soil that

has been tracked in.

6. When you go hiking, a pebble will find its way into your boot.

7. Yes, you are the only family sleeping in the woods.

8. Given a chance, matches will find a way to get wet.

9. Matches don't work in the woods.

10. When something is labeled "waterproof," be forewarned. It doesn't keep the water out but will do a perfect job of keeping the sweat in.

11. Tent stakes are made of the softest metal known to man.

12. Mosquitoes only show up when you run out of repellent.

13. Tents can never go back into the box in which they came.

14. It's almost impossible to distinguish between freeze-dried food and dog food.

15. For every night you camp out, you will

have one less tent stake than the night before.

16. At least once a night, the tent lines will come close to beheading someone.

17. Hammocks are for professionals. Don't try using them on your own.

18. No matter which side of the campfire you face, the smoke will always drift your way.

19. Living in a tent for a week with your family will cause you to change your mind about buying a tiny house.

20. No matter what kind of clothes you bring, they're sure to be the wrong ones.

21. The "Embrace Nature, Go Camping" campaign was started by the Motel Association.

22. The farther you go into the woods, the less well the wood will burn.

23. All the bad things that happen will become what you brag about when you return home. "Remember the night the gale-force winds came, and each kid held down a corner

of the tent?"

24. You get to see the stars as never before and realize the greatness of our God.

25. But the best thing about camping is that you did it all with your family.

I don't know if Mary and Joseph ever took Jesus camping; the Bible doesn't say. Did Jesus grow up in a tent?

I don't know, but the Bible does have a lot to say about family. The fifth commandment says to "Honor your father and your mother" (Ex. 20:12). And when Joshua took over after Moses died, he announced to the country of Israel, "But as for me and my household, we will serve the Lord" (Josh. 24:15b).

But the Bible has much more to say about husbands, wives, and children. It is a book about family and how to survive (in my case, anyway) the challenges of camping.

===

Did you know Jesus enlarged the concept of family?

===

One day, He was speaking to a crowd and was told his mother and brothers wanted to talk to him. Our Lord used this moment to recast the definition of family: "For whoever does the will of my Father in heaven is my brother and sister and mother" (Matt. 12:50).

I realize some of you may feel as though you don't have a family. But if you're a follower of Jesus, you belong to one that will be yours for eternity. Just let me give you one piece of advice: Don't let them take you camping.

No Gouda

I love cheese—all kinds of cheese. Since I am from Oklahoma, home of Will Rogers, I can say I have never met a cheese I didn't like. I am a cheese-lover, so I get excited when my work takes me to the Netherlands, the cheese capital of the world. Stores there sell cheese in every size, shape, and flavor.

One day while ministering in this cheese-loving country, I decided to buy one of those big, round, wax-coated wheels of gouda to bring back home. I made my choice and carefully carried the huge cheese all the way to Tulsa on the plane.

I did not realize my purchase would set me up for a big disappointment. I had planned to divide the gouda and give it to my coworkers and friends. Instead, I found that I couldn't even make a dent in it. That wheel of cheese was as hard as my youngest son's head. Even the amazing knife we had bought at the state fair couldn't put a mark on it.

I hacked; I sawed; I even chopped, but it wouldn't budge.

Finally, I threw the entire wheel of cheese away.

On my next trip to the Netherlands, still fuming about that terrible cheese, I went back to the store where I bought it. I told the owner that the Gouda he had sold me was no good.

He asked what was wrong. I begin to describe to him all the ways I had found to torture the cheese—that the only thing I hadn't tried in an attempt to cut his rock-hard Gouda was my chainsaw. As I continued talking, I could sense his irritation.

When I finished, he said simply, "You dumb American! What you bought was aged Gouda." He went on to explain that this type of cheese is cured for a long time. The more it ages, the more expensive it gets. As gouda ages, it becomes parmesan. That's the cheese you sprinkle on top of your spaghetti or pizza. The man also told me that instead of trying to cut or slice the valuable cheese, I should have carefully grated it.

No wonder he was infuriated. In my ignorance, I had

taken something he had nurtured and crafted into some of the finest cheese in the world and thrown it into the trash can.

I sometimes find parallels in my life to the gouda incident.

God has created wonderful friends, family members, and coworkers for me, but I seem to forget how precious they are.

Relationships, like the finest cheese, should become more valuable and precious over time. But it seems many people are like me. Often, we trash those who are the closest to us.

Take the time to evaluate and recognize the value of the people God has brought into your life.

Then, remind them just how gouda they are.

Jesus Loves Me

"Jesus Loves Me" is one of the first songs I can remember learning as a kid. You should have seen me in the front row of the preschool choir, my parents looking on with great anticipation. I was one of those little boys who wasn't afraid to lean back on his heels and let the music rip from the bottom of his tiny heart. I sang as though I were the guest soloist for the church cantata, and the rest of the children were there only as my backup singers.

When I got to the chorus, I sang with all the gusto a four-year-old could muster, "Yes, Jesus loves me, Yes, Jesus loves me, Yes, Jesus loves me, The Bible teeellls-meee-soooo." .

(My flair for the dramatic led me to hold out the last few words for emphasis every time)

The problem was, I could sing it—but I couldn't believe it. "Jesus loves me" must be one of the most difficult theological concepts for anyone to understand.

Another song reminded me of that one, but it sounded a little different. This was the one about "Jesus Loves the Little Children of The World." Again, I sang boldly, "Red and yellow, black and white, they are precious in His sight." Now this song, I could sing and believe. I believed God loved the children starving in Ethiopia and the children running through the jungles of Panama. He loved the orphaned children in faraway China and the city kids on the busy streets of Manhattan. In fact, I believed He loved all the children of the world—except one. I also believe many of you who read this know who that one is. You see that person every day in the mirror.

The children who sing those songs grow up to be adults who serve in the church. We greet each other in the hallways and say, "God bless you." Now, I can hand out "God bless yous" all day long and come home feeling good about myself, but take it literally that God wants to bless me? I'm not so sure about that. After all, if I'm not even convinced that Jesus loves me, how can I be sure He wants to bless me?

When I was a child, I needed a real Jesus, not the Jesus

in a song. I needed a Jesus with arms that could hold me close when I was afraid, a Jesus who could run his fingers through my hair and whisper that it was going to be all right. I needed a Jesus who wasn't stuck in a stained- glass window or fixed to a cross hanging on a wall. I needed a Jesus who would play baseball with me when nobody else would bother. I needed a Jesus who would laugh at my childish jokes and join me in a game of Hide 'n Seek. I needed a Jesus who would lie beside me at night when I went to sleep and who would already be awake when I got up in the morning. I needed a Jesus who would join me in burping contests and, with laughter in His voice, let me win. I needed a Jesus who would let me crawl up into His lap, looking deep and long into His eyes to find only acceptance. I needed a real Jesus.

How could Jesus do all these things for me? Through His body: the church.

Jesus put special people in His church to interact with me as a child.

These parts of His body helped me begin to understand the real Jesus. One was the Royal Ambassador leader who put up a tent in the church backyard and made us all into

Native Americans. We learned how Jesus loved them, and when I took off those markings, the leader who loved me with paint on my face would still love the little boy who was just me.

Another part of Jesus's body was my favorite Sunday school teacher. Every time he saw me, he reminded me he knew I would become someone special. When I looked in his eyes, I believed him. Still another was my pastor who let me call him "Brother Harry" and took me once a week to Dairy Queen, handing me a dime to buy anything on the menu that I wanted.

Jesus did love me! One person was His arm, another His hand, and another His heart. When I put them all together, I saw Jesus.

This week, what part of Jesus will a child see in you?

Dumb Questions

You've heard it, I've heard it: "There is no such thing as a dumb question."

Those who say this have never had children. Anyone who has children knows dumb questions abound. How many times have I heard my two sons ask, "Are we there yet?" I was always tempted to answer, "No, I'm just driving around in circles till you quit asking."

My youngest son once asked Cathy and me, "When are you going to get a divorce?"

He had come to the conclusion that all his classmates who were products of divorce had it far better than he did. They got two birthday parties and two Christmases. If the parents remarried, the number of grandparents doubled. Of course, the more grandparents you have, the more stuff you get.

There are many questions that should be asked. There

are some that should not. Allow me to give you a few examples. People tell me, "A stitch in time saves nine." Saves nine what? Before they invented drawing boards, what did people go back to? If crime doesn't pay, does that mean my job is a crime? Can you get cavities in your dentures if you use too much artificial sweetener? Why does an iron have a setting for "permanent press"?

How do they put the "Keep off the Grass" signs on the lawn? How do you get off a non-stop flight? Where in the nursery rhyme does it say Humpty Dumpty was an egg, anyway?

Why isn't "phonetic" spelled the way it sounds?

Why do we call it a "building" when it is already built? Why do we consider "clear" a color? Why does it take fifteen minutes to cook Minute Rice? Why do we say something is "out of whack"? For that matter, what is a "whack"?

How did a fool and his money get together? If the No. 2 pencil is the most popular, why is it still No. 2? Why do people tell you when they are speechless?

Do pilots take crash courses? Why do we say it's a "free gift"? Aren't all gifts free? Do vegetarians eat animal crackers? Why aren't wrong numbers ever busy? Why can't we tickle ourselves? When the clock was first invented, how did they know what time it was so they could set it? Why does Hawaii have interstate highways? If Barbie is so popular, why do you have to buy all her friends?

Why is lemon juice made with artificial flavoring and dishwashing liquid with real lemons? Why is the third hand on a watch called a "second hand"? Where does your lap go when you stand up? How did the man who invented cottage cheese know he was done? These are the real questions people should ask.

> One thing we know about Jesus as a young man is that He asked the right questions.

Scripture tells us, "After three days they found him in the temple courts, sitting among the teachers, listening to them and asking them questions. Everyone who heard him was amazed at his understanding and his answers" (Luke 2:46-47).

I bet Jesus wasn't asking questions like, "Who killed the Dead Sea?" or "Who is buried in Abraham's tomb?" The Bible doesn't give us any clues about what He asked as a twelve-year-old boy, but we do know that as an adult, He asked many thought-provoking questions. One day after Jesus had healed a paralytic man, He told him, "Son, your sins are forgiven" (Mark 2:5b). The scribes really thought they had Him then. When they confronted Him, He turned the tables by asking them a simple question, "Which is easier: to say to the paralytic, 'Your sins are forgiven,' or to say, 'Get up, take your mat and walk?'" (Mark 2:9). I can almost imagine the looks on their faces as they stood there, speechless.

On another day, Jesus' disciples were discussing who He was. He turned to them and said, "Who do you say I am?" (Matt 16:15). An entire sermon lies within that question. It really doesn't matter what others think or say about Jesus. Who do you think, believe, and say He is?

If you want to do an interesting Bible study someday, underline all the questions Jesus asked. You'll discover the same thing I did: Jesus had a ministry of asking questions.

When your children ask dumb things like, "What do people who live in China call their good dishes?" or "What hair color do they list on the driver's license of a bald man?" keep praying about them and their questions.

One of these days, they'll ask the right ones.

Garage Sale Lessons

Garage sales are demonic. Maybe not demonic, but they can't be more than a step from the edge of the abyss. No one in his right (or even his left) mind would hold a garage sale without the evil influence of a force from below.

I'm blowing off steam because my wife has announced an upcoming sale at a garage close to ours. Have we lost our minds? I am seriously—very seriously—praying for the return of our Lord before that eventful day.

Sure, I regularly run into friends who tell me they just held a garage sale that earned over a thousand dollars in eight hours. If I remember correctly (and these are the kind of memories I try to repress), when we did our last garage sale, I spent eight hours the night before putting out signs, stacking all kinds of stuff on four-by-eight sheets of plywood, and covering them with a sheet so we would be ready to go in the morning.

Garage sales bring out interesting people. The first to arrive are the ones who can't read. The signs clearly state "8:00 a.m. – 5:00 p.m.," but

---

You're awakened at six thirty by a group of illiterate people walking around your driveway.

They may not know how to read, but they can talk— loudly. And they have no problem ringing your doorbell at 6:00 a.m. to ask if you'll take ten dollars for the table that holds all those bargains.

I get it now, though. My wife informed me that these illiterate-loud talkers are actually "fulltime, hardcore, serious garage-sale hoppers." I knew little about this human subspecies. Apparently, they do this hopping every weekend. They plot a course, begin early in the morning, and hit as many garage sales as they can.

After sitting in the sun for hours watching throngs of people go through our junk to barter a dime item down to a nickel, I realized something important. For the garage-sale addicts, the thrill comes not in the item to be bought but in seeing how close they can come to getting someone else's junk free. No one intends to pay the prices scrawled on the masking tape. The art of negotiation is at its best (or at least its most intense) during a garage sale. I have a tip for the federal government: Have these garage-sale hoppers conduct our country's negotiations with foreign countries. The government doesn't exist that could withstand this kind of pressure!

At our last garage sale, I spent hours watching people pay their dimes and walk away grinning as though they had won the lottery. When everything ended, I was thankful they were gone. We made something like $48.92. If you deduct the sheets of plywood, the Cokes I drank, and our Whataburger lunch, I figure we cleared about eighty-three cents. I'm trying to convince my wife that this time, we'll call Goodwill and have them haul our stuff away. I'll lose eighty-three cents and an aching back, but I'll regain that precious two hours of sleep.

I wonder if Joseph felt like a garage-sale item when his brothers stuck him in a hole and sold him into slavery.

Satan always wants to come along and devalue what God has deemed valuable.

Can I tell you a secret? You matter to God. You are priceless. I have been making a list of all the people in Scripture who matter to God. You won't believe the ones He considers important: blind people, diseased people, demon-possessed people, dead people, grieving people, hurting people, troubled people, and religious people. As I reread the story of the cross, I realized that thieves and murderers matter. Everybody matters to God. And that includes you.

Many of you who read this have bought into Satan's lies. You feel like a garage-sale item. But God the Father sent his Son Jesus to take the things the world has deemed non-valuable and redeem them with His shed blood. "But God chose the foolish things of the world to shame the wise; God chose the weak things of the world to shame the strong" (1 Cor. 1:27).

Do your children feel non-valuable? Look into their eyes, use their first names, and tell them the truth: They matter to God. Joseph knew he was more than a garage-sale item. He endured pain, but his life gloriously displays God's power and purpose.

When our sale finally ended, I asked my wife what to do with our eighty-three cents. She wanted to take it and go to a garage sale.

Time and Treasures

Time is a beast that will either chase you toward or away from the better things.

When I was young, television was just coming into its own. I spent the early part of my life listening to radio. To this day, I would rather listen to the radio than watch television. With the radio, you can do other things: build model cars, sand a tabletop, or work on a puzzle. But television takes these options away from you.

As a young man, I worked as a photographer. This was back in the days before we had heard the word "digital." I worked in a small darkroom with one dim red light for hours on end, developing negatives and processing prints. But even there, I was never alone. My constant companion was the music pumped in by WHB of Kansas City. The DJs who cranked out the top-40 hits called themselves the World's Happiest Broadcasters. The radio station followed me home, where I lay in bed at night, smiling as I waited for the gravelly howls of Wolfman Jack and sure that life was good.

Looking back, I'm stunned by what I used to deem important and by the things I treasured. I don't know if we all go through this process, but God has used time to point me to the more valuable things of life.

I don't treasure possessions the way I used to, unless you count my highly prized 45 rpm "Love Potion No. Nine" record.

(Some of us will have to explain to this digital generation the difference between 33 1/3s and 45s.)

These days, I treasure time. I treasure the time I have with my wife, my sons, and especially our newest addition: our first grandson, Titus. I don't understand how time has slipped through my fingers. Only yesterday, I was goggle-eyeing one of the most beautiful girls I had ever seen, and soon, she and I will celebrate forty years of marriage.

I have become a time-grabber. I grab every minute I can with any of my family members. I treasure our short rides to the grocery store. I treasure the conversation as they talk about whatever they want. The topic doesn't matter to me because I cherish the time more than the conversation.

I treasure friendships, old and new. Time has taught me that friendships are the spice rack of life. Some of them you use every day and others, only on occasion, but they are nice to have when needed. Time has not only taught me the value of having friends, but of being a friend. When someone needs me, I'm not in as much of a hurry as I was in the past. Over the years, I've learned that the things I thought were demanding and important will still be demanding and important next week.

Time has taught me to treasure the Word of God, and I've seen the importance of meditating on it. It has truly become the lamp for my feet and the light for my path (see Ps. 119:105). As I've seen God deliver on His promises, the Bible has become even more relevant. I've instructed my family that if our house catches on fire, they should first make sure everyone gets out safely and second, they should retrieve my Bible. It is worn, marked-up, and has pages falling out, but it holds the sacred truths of life.

All in all, time has taught me to treasure two things. First, I have learned to treasure relationships above worldly things. But I still have lots of things I hold dear. Old yellowed papers with pictures my sons drew in school, the word "Dad" scrawled below them in crayon, or a page with their first wobbly rendering of the words, "I love you." The Hopalong Cassidy cereal bowl and plate my departed mother bought me as a young child. The pictures of my family and the many Christmases, vacations, and school activities we enjoyed together. I value these items, but I treasure the relationships with my family and friends more.

Time has also taught me to treasure the things of God.

God Himself, His Word, the church, brothers and sisters in Christ, the community of believers working life out together, the preaching of the Word, and missions—all of these grow more and more valuable to me.

I guess what I want to say to all young people is to take it from those of who are closer to the end of the road than you. Let time take you not to the good things of life but to the best: God and relationships.

"There is a time for everything, and a season for every activity under the heavens" (Eccl. 3:1).

Travel Tips

I'm writing from Máncora, Peru, one of the many places where I work that no one has ever heard of. I could pretend to be writing from Paris, but the empanada stands, lilting pan flute music, and Spanish street signs won't let me forget where I am.

You can't get to this place from where you live, and if you're here, you're probably lost. I just returned from the tourist market, taking a little break from teaching and getting a little exercise in the process. I passed the usual hawkers trying to entice me to buy something from their booths. I thought I should share some of the knowledge gained in my years of travel that might benefit you if you ever visit a place like this.

First, you should know there is only one size of clothing outside the United States: small.

Don't even ask if they have an extra-large or a double extra-large. They may carry them, but they're the same size with different tags.

"Do you have that in extra-large?"

"Yes, my friend, we carry all sizes for special people like you." The man brings out an extra large and lays it next to the small. They look identical. "Those are the same size."

"Yes, sir, they do look the same, but looks can be deceiving, my friend. See the tags? This one says 'small' and this one says, 'extra-large.'" As he talks, he is stretching the shirt to make it bigger. He then holds it against my body, and I can tell it's about three sizes too small. "Sir, this is a perfect fit for a man of your build."

I think, *Well, I have lost a little weight, and this guy's an expert on T-shirts.* So I buy it. It now sits in a pile with the rest of my "looks can be deceiving" shirts.

I should tell you one more things about buying clothes outside the country. If they do happen to have an actual extra-large T-shirt, the size is temporary. As soon as you wash it, it will shrink down to join the rest of your too-small shirts. If you wear a size small, the world is yours. If you're larger, make sure you have a small friend you can bless.

The second thing you should know is to leave your watch home, unless you're going to Switzerland (in which case you need to take a stopwatch). Most of the world doesn't know how to tell time. The bus comes when it comes and goes when it goes, and everything else follows that pattern. Forget reading timetables or anything else with a time designation.

I once went to the movies in Peru, and the show was supposed to start at 7 p.m. But at seven o'clock, nothing happened, and it seemed like no one cared. One man got up, banged on the back wall and sat back down. A few minutes later, several more people got up and did the same. Ten minutes later, half the theater banged on the back wall, and the movie started. I found out later that they only begin a movie when enough patrons bang on the wall. I tried this in our home theater. It didn't work.

The need to forget your watch overseas applies especially to meetings. I was fortunate today; my 9 a.m. class started at 10:30 a.m., and my lunch was at 2 p.m.

And when you're overseas, distance is the close cousin to time.

It's almost impossible in another country to find out how far one place is from another or how long you must travel to reach it.

I was in Africa a while back, and they told me our next stop was a mile and a half down the road. Three hours later, I asked, "I thought we were just going a mile and a half?"

"Yes, sir, we are. It's just a few minutes away."

Six hours later, we reached our destination. I can't prove it, but I'm pretty sure the guy in Peru who sold me the extra-large T-shirt and the guy in Africa who informed me our destination was a mile and a half down the road are cousins. I'm also pretty sure they called each other and had a good laugh at my expense.

Those who intend to work in other countries should take the advice of the apostle Paul. "I have become all things to all people so that by all possible means I might save some" (1 Cor. 9:22b). Who knows? You may even find it liberating not to be bound by time or distance.

I need to go. It's 9:30 p.m., and my seven o'clock class will start soon.

O Come, Let Us Ignore Him

Have you experienced it yet? Sooner or later, it comes to all parents: that one fleeting moment when you feel tremendous pride in your children—until the next instant, when they open their tiny mouths and take it all away.

Cathy and I have never lived close to our families. When we married, we left her little hometown of Hannibal, Missouri, and moved to Quitman, Texas; then to Mesquite, Texas; finally ending up in Tulsa, where we have lived for the past twenty-five years. I served on a church staff most of our married life, so I only got a week or two off every year. We spent nearly every vacation visiting either her parents or mine.

One Christmas, we arrived at her parents' home just in time to go with them to their little church's children's Christmas program. I realize that some readers may not fully understand the differences between a small church's Christmas program and that of a large church. In a large church, the children's Christmas program is an event. In a small church, it is a program. A large church has multiple rehearsals, costumes, props, and backgrounds called sets. Sometimes, these sets are scale reproductions of the entire city of Bethlehem.

In a large church, the children have racks of costumes from which to choose, all authentic period reproductions. In a small church, the children are draped in sheets. Mary and Joseph get the new blue ones and the angels don the slightly used, semi-white ones. Other props include a plastic baby Jesus and halos made of pipe cleaners.

Have you noticed that halos and children never go together well?

No matter how they're attached, something always seems to slip.

The props for a small church's children's Christmas program include a bale of hay borrowed from Uncle Fred's barn. He needs it back right away so his horses can eat. In a small church program, the background consists of several sheets sewn together and painted to depict the hills of Jerusalem. In 1972, Aunt Harriet took a Holy Land Tour called, "Running Where Jesus Walked." Naturally, when the Children's Christmas Program Committee needed someone to paint the background sheets, the vote was unanimous that Aunt Harriet do the honors. She wasn't a very good painter, but she was the only one who had a clue what the real hills looked like.

In a large church, you are greeted at the door and handed a professionally printed, four-color program listing each child's name and part. Below the children's names is a list of auxiliary personnel including set designers, costume designer, program designer, and a special thanks to the caterer. In a small church, a teenage usher hands you a bulletin run off on a forty-year-old mimeograph machine, leaving an inky smell lingering in the air. The large-church children's Christmas program uses live animals. In a small church, the children smell somewhat like animals. When a large-church program is about to begin, the lights dim, the kettle drum rolls, and a spotlight encircles Mary and Joseph as they begin their trek across Bethlehem.

In a small church, if Grandma and Grandpa happen to bring a grandchild that night, the Christmas program gains a new participant.

After all, nothing pleases grandparents more than seeing their grandchildren up on stage during a Christmas program.

And that, my friends, is right where the Moore family found ourselves on that Christmas long ago. Naturally, Cathy's parents had done their share of bragging about our children taking part in our large-church children's Christmas program (excuse me; I mean *event*). And of course, these proud grandparents wanted our youngest son to sing the song he sang there. Obediently, he got up to perform. My chest began to swell. Deep in my heart, I knew his large-church training would make him the star of the show.

Valiantly, he began to sing, "O, Come, All Ye Faithful." I could tell by his face, though, that something wasn't quite right. He couldn't remember all the words. With a large-church voice, he reached the chorus, "O come let us ignore him. O Come, let us ignore Him. . . " At about this time, I was looking for a pew to hide under.

I had to give him credit. After all, the words "ignore" and "adore" do sound much the same. But that's where the similarity ends.

Yes, our son was the hit of the small church children's program—for all the wrong reasons. As we enter this season of honoring our Savior sent to "dwell among men," which will your life reflect: adore or ignore?

Oh come, let us adore Him—today.

Red Sea or Gethsemane?

When I was a child, my family attended a small country church. You've seen dozens like it. This white-framed wooden building was surrounded by a cemetery. I guess the congregation wanted to be as close as possible to the resurrection of the dead.

The thing I remember most about the church, though, was not its cemetery, but its prayer life. These people prayed all the time.

I don't mean the type of prayer meetings we see in our churches today, but an entire congregation broken and weeping as people took their requests before the Lord.

This thing called prayer has always confused me. Sometimes I pray, and God moves heaven and earth on my behalf. At other times, prayer feels as if I'm tossing bricks skyward. My petitions don't travel far before they come crashing down. And I realize many of you have prayed for years without feeling as though God hears you.

Over the past few months, God has been teaching me that our prayers end up in one of two places. The first is the Red Sea. Think back to Exodus, when Moses was bringing the Israelites out of the Promised Land. There in the wilderness, he encountered an insurmountable problem. I believe this experience shows us the Bible's first Baptists. How do we know they were Baptists? Simple. They whined and complained that they would have been better off if Moses had left them to die in Egypt.

> Moses, already a wise leader, told his crabby crew to wait and see what great things God would do.

And you know the rest of the story. God parted the Red Sea, and Moses and the grumpy Baptists—excuse me, Israelites—crossed in safety.

Red Sea prayers end with God changing the external. As a missionary, I've often witnessed the results of prayers like these. For example, our ministry has never asked for money. Instead, we pray and leave our requests at God's doorstep. One day we needed $5,000. My wife and I were in the back of our office, praying, when we heard someone at the front door yelling, "I'm a delivery boy from God!"

We ran up to check out the commotion, and there on the ground was a plain, unmarked envelope. We opened it to find the exact amount of money we needed. Our prayers ended in the Red Sea, where God moved external circumstances to meet our needs. But not all prayers are answered this way.

King David didn't get the answer he wanted when his son became ill. For seven days he prayed and asked God to heal the infant boy, but his son died anyway. And when Paul asked God to remove his thorn in the flesh, the Lord didn't do that, either.

Even Jesus, in Matthew 26, asked God if it would be possible to remove the cross. This is the only time in Scripture we see Jesus repeat a prayer. Three times, He asked His heavenly Father if He had an alternate plan. But God didn't give Him one.

All these prayers ended up not in the Red Sea, but in Gethsemane.

A Red Sea prayer changes external circumstances. A Gethsemane prayer changes you.

Instead of changing the external, a Gethsemane prayer changes the internal.

The Gethsemane prayer changed King David. He rose from his prayer to worship God. The Gethsemane prayer also changed Paul. He realized the thorn in his flesh was meant to keep him humble. And of course, the Gethsemane prayer changed Jesus. Each time He prayed, He moved from "Let this cup be removed" to "Thy kingdom come; Thy will be done."

All prayers end in one of two places: the Red Sea, where God does an incredible thing and changes the external, or Gethsemane, where He changes the internal.

Jesus says in Luke 9:23 that we must deny ourselves, take up our cross daily and follow Him. Unless you pass through Gethsemane, you can't reach the cross.

Which is the greater prayer: Red Sea or Gethsemane? I believe the Gethsemane prayer has more power, because a changed life changes lives.

Not long ago, I took one more step in learning to pray like our Lord. Our prayers begin with surrender when we go to our knees. But they also end with surrender when we tell our heavenly Father, "Thy will be done. "

When I pray, I don't know whether God will take my prayer to the Red Sea, where I can stand by and watch His glory, or to Gethsemane, where His glory is revealed in me. But I do know what I desire most: His kingdom come, His will be done. And as long as He is with me, He can take my prayers—and me—wherever He thinks best.

Culture Shock

My mother made me do it. Every week for four long years, she dragged my brother and me to piano lessons. When all my friends were outside playing baseball, I found myself hunched over a broken-down piano, running scales.

My piano teacher was an elderly spinster who believed God's call on her life was to teach every child to be a concert pianist. If she had anything to do with it, you would never leave her class until you had performed at Carnegie Hall. To this day, I believe she would have made a great piano teacher . . . for the Marines.

During my lessons, this teacher sat beside me with a yellow pencil that sported a giant square eraser. Every time I missed a note, she used the pencil to whack my knuckles. To this day, when I see a pencil with an oversized eraser, I break out in chills and a cold sweat.

For the Moore boys, piano lessons and weekly torture were one and the same experience.

You see, even though we lived out in the country, my mom was determined to introduce her sons to culture. At church, she enrolled us in Royal Ambassadors. There, while we learned about the need to share Jesus, we studied different ways of life and people all over the world. Mom also read aloud to us and made sure we had plenty of books to read on our own. Despite her efforts, I never became a true "artsy" type—just a missionary who still loves to read. If it were not for my wife's good taste, our home would probably be decorated in velvet pictures of Elvis. Once, I stood in line to see the Mona Lisa, and I was disappointed when I realized it was only the size of a piece of notebook paper. When I go to a museum, I enjoy watching the other visitors much more than studying the paintings or statues.

Despite it all, I follow my mom's example in many ways. On the mission field, we always try to introduce our students to the culture of the country in which we are working. A crucial part of missionary service is understanding and immersing oneself in the culture as much as possible.

We tell our students that an in-depth cultural education always carries with it additional opportunities to share Christ.

On one mission experience, I took a team of students to Hungary for five weeks. Have you ever seen a Future Farmer of America (FFA) from Mustang, Oklahoma, sitting through the Royal Ballet performance of Tchaikovsky's "Sleeping Beauty?" As we say in Oklahoma, it's like a calf looking at a new gate.

I always enjoy watching the students' faces as they experience new aspects of culture. At first, their eyes scan from side to side, hoping desperately that none of their classmates from the United States is within a thousand miles. Picture it: strapping young FFA students sitting in the gilded 1883 Opera House watching the ballet. At first, they are bewildered by the male dancers running on tiptoe and leaping across the stage in their cabbage-green tights. For most of the students, that image alone proves quite a shock. Gradually, though, they begin to get caught up in the magic of the story and the music.

It's a funny thing, though. Most of the cultural learning seems to stay in the host country. If we asked them today, most of these students would probably not want to reveal that they attended such a performance, and they especially would not want anyone to know they enjoyed it.

Still, the discipline a child gains from participating in and experiencing cultural activities is extremely valuable. Does your child need to become a famous sculptor or a musical virtuoso? Probably not. Should your child gain an appreciation for the arts? Almost certainly. I find that today's children know more about video games and sports than octaves and middle C. I highly recommend that you expose your child to a play, opera, or ballet. The experience will enrich their lives, and who knows? You might even save them from a shock when they travel to the mission field someday.

Dear Father, when I look at Your artwork, I am in complete awe. The way You stretched the clouds across a deep blue canvas speaks of Your unending love. The brilliant glory of the sun speaks to the glory we will see when we look upon You. The multihued greens in the grass, flowers, and leaves remind me of Your unfathomable depths. Thank You for Your faithfulness. Help me as I teach my child to see and to appreciate You in nature and in art. Amen.

Real Men Don't Cry

I am not a crier, I am not a crier, I AM NOT A CRIER!

Well, you might say I cry on occasion. To be honest, I find myself crying a lot more than I used to. I grew up in the era when the mantra for training young boys was, "Real men don't cry." This was usually followed by those three words of wise counsel, "Suck it up." I don't know how many times I heard my dad tell me, "Real men don't cry."

Looking back on my life, I understand what he was trying to teach me. You can't cry over everything.

He was right; some events don't require a flood from the five frontal orifices of your head

(as a child, I used to slobber and blow snot whenever I cried).

Recently, I find myself crying over things I never thought would move me. I'm watching an AT & T commercial where a dad leaves on a business trip. He gets into the taxicab and opens his briefcase to find one of his daughter's stuffed animals.

I catch a deep breath and blink, but I stop as soon as I hear the voice inside my head. It whispers, *Real men don't cry.* The commercial continues with the dad in London. He holds up the stuffed animal and takes its picture in front of Big Ben so he can send it to his little girl. She squeals with delight when she sees the image.

This time, I take two deep breaths, my heart pounds harder, and I feel my nose begin to run. Next, the dad sends a picture from Paris with his daughter's stuffed animal in front of the Eiffel Tower. My eyes must have sprung a leak, but I remain in control, repeating to myself, "Real men don't cry; real men don't cry."

The commercial ends with the dad sending one more photo to his daughter. It shows the stuffed animal sitting in front of their house. All at once, the little girl realizes what this means. She runs to the door, swings it wide, and runs to hug her dad.

By now, I'm a basket case. I can't hold it in any longer. I slobber and blow snot as I rejoice over the love of this family. Yes, I know it's only a commercial, but something inside me desires that love for my own family and every other family, too. I also feel guilty—because I cried.

I wonder if Joseph ever told Jesus, "Real men don't cry" or "Suck it up." I have always imagined Jesus as a man's man. Since He worked as a carpenter most of His life, I imagine His body as well-toned from chiseling and scraping all that wood. I imagine His hands as callused, the labor of life ingrained into the crevices of His palms. And I imagine him as physically strong, since He was able to survive without food for forty days and nights.

But there are some things about Jesus I don't have to imagine. I don't have to imagine His sensitivity to the rejects of society, for I read about His encounter with a woman at the well. I don't have to imagine His compassion for the disabled. He told the lame man to take up his pallet and walk, and the man was healed. I don't have to imagine Jesus' respect for women, because they loved Him so much they came to the empty tomb before anyone else. I don't have to imagine Jesus' love for children, because He told each of us to approach him as a little child. And I don't have to imagine Jesus crying, because I know He wept over the city of Jerusalem, the city of peace that rejected the King of Peace. He wept over his friend Lazarus' death.

And sometimes, I believe He weeps over me.

As my years of being a Christ-follower continue, I find myself crying more and more. I cry over the lack of missionaries; the harvest is plentiful but the laborers are few. I cry over dysfunctional families. I cry over a man who stands on the side of the road with a sign that says, "Will work for food." And I have discovered that real men cry after all.

Yes, Dad, real men cry. They cry over the things that break the heart of God. They can cry without feeling guilt. They don't have to "suck it up" if they are following our Savior's example, because the Bible says, "Jesus wept" (John 11:35).

Piece of Work

For my birthday last year, my wife gave me a custom-made T-shirt. Some special words march across its front: "I am a piece of work."

I'm not sure where she got this line, but she never says it in a derogatory way. Instead, she applies it to me whenever I can't do something she thought I could. Like many wives, her high expectations don't always match her husband's abilities.

I am fairly handy around the house. This means I can do a little carpentry, plumbing, and electrical work. The problem comes because my loving wife believes I can do it all. "After you finish painting the bedroom, why don't you put a new foundation under our house?" "After you rotate the tires, will you put in a new transmission?" Sometimes she volunteers me to help other people. I am honored by her confidence, but I usually know where to draw the line.

The other day, my niece brought over her car so I could help replace a thermostat. Now, I have replaced many of these in my lifetime. The procedure is simple: remove two bolts, pull out the old thermostat, install the new one, and replace the bolts. But when I opened the hood of my niece's car, the engine looked different than anything I've ever seen.

First, the thermostat was not secured by two bolts but by three odd-looking screws. These screw heads contained no screwdriver slots. In fact, they looked as though someone had reamed out the inside of each one. If you could shrink the Pentagon down to the size of an M & M, it would fit perfectly inside one of these strange screws.

The other problem was that the thermostat wasn't located on top of the engine but somewhere between there and China. Since I didn't have the proper tool to remove those weird screws (I later learned the proper name, "torque bolts"), I made a trip to the parts store. The salesman asked me what size I needed. I explained I had to remove three bolts that looked like the Pentagon shrunk down to the size of an M & M. For some reason, the parts-store people didn't speak my language. They didn't want to know about M & Ms; they wanted to know what millimeter bolt I meant.

Since I was born before the 1970s, I know nothing about metric measurements.

> My generation got rid of the metric system at the same time as we threw the tea into the Boston Harbor.

As far as I'm concerned, millimeters, kilograms, and kilometers ought to be taught under the heading, "Foreign Languages."

The parts-store salesman told me if I knew the millimeter size of the bolt, I could buy a single torque driver for about $4. Since I didn't know that measurement, I would have to buy a $55 kit that contained every size torque wrench known to mankind. Apparently, that's their standard penalty for those of us who are metric-ignorant.

I returned from the parts store and told the ladies-in-waiting I wouldn't be able to fix the thermostat. That's when I heard it: "You're a piece of work."

I'm glad my wife sees me as a person who can do great things. When she does this, she's acting like God. Throughout history, He changed people's names to reflect

His expectations. Abram became Abraham, Sarai became Sarah, Simon became Peter, and the list goes on.

But Jesus changed more than names; He changed people's character, too.

He took someone like Simon Barjona and told him, "I don't see you as having the qualities of a Simon. I see you more like a rock." Jesus renamed him as Peter to recast his identity.

I have discovered over my years of ministry that I can do what Jesus did. I once took a young boy named Michael overseas. He jumped every time I said his name. I realized he associated that name with the "I can't do anything right" mentality.

Soon, I bought him a bracelet inscribed "Michael Paul." I sat him down and told him, "From now on, I will call you 'Michael Paul' because I see in you more of Paul's characteristics than Michael's."

I then explained what I meant. Do you know what happened? I've never seen a student make such a turnaround. He began to walk with confidence. He found a boldness he had never known. And the next summer,

Michael Paul returned as the team leader.

What you call a person sets up an expectation to fulfill. Give your children names they can grow into. If the name you choose calls forth positive character qualities, in the end, they will become a piece of work: His.

Jesus' Favorite Child

Recently, I had the privilege of speaking at First Baptist Church, McCloud, Oklahoma, a tremendously warm and welcoming place. I arrived early to record a radio interview. After the interview ended, I needed to go out to my truck.

As I returned and walked into the sanctuary, I saw a lady sitting on the back row, sniffling. I didn't think much about it until I began hearing a few sobs interjected with the sniffles. I was walking toward her when she looked up and asked if I was a minister. I told her I was, asked how I could help, and she told me her story.

This lady hadn't been to church in years. She was involved in a relationship that was very difficult, but something had been prompting her to come to church. She kept repeating, "Something told me to come here tonight, and I don't know why."

I looked her in the eye and said, "I know why. Jesus wants me to tell you something: You are His favorite child."

"I am?" she responded.

I began to tell her she was wonderfully made—that even before the foundation of the world, God drew up a blueprint for her life. When she heard this good news, she began to sob. She stayed for the service, and the church surrounded her with love and grace.

The enemy delights in trying to give us the spirit of an orphan. An orphan has no father, no home. When Satan rebelled against God, he chose to become the first orphan, destined to roam the earth.

As a missionary, I have spent many days working in orphanages. I also know some orphans who have been adopted. Even though they now have homes and loving parents, some of them retain this orphan spirit. They are afraid to trust. They have been hurt in the past, and they are afraid it will happen again. They are afraid of intimacy. They keep their hearts guarded. They hurt the ones who love them the most. Just the other day, someone asked me for advice about a person who was adopted but rejected his adoptive parents when he got older.

What did Satan do when he became an orphan? He

began working to trick others into thinking they were orphans, too. He went to Adam and Eve, who had a wonderful home, and planted doubts in their mind about their loving heavenly Father. They bought into these lies. Soon, they found themselves turned out of their home, estranged from their Father.

Jesus says in John 14:18a, "I will not leave you as orphans." He knew an orphan spirit would cause his children to say, "Because I have no father, I have no identity. If I have no identity, I have no destiny. If have no destiny, I have no direction. If I have no direction, I have no purpose. If I have no purpose, I have no life."

What did Jesus come to give us? Life, abundant life! But we only have that abundant life when we have sonship. We need to remember He has adopted us and loves us more than any earthly father or mother ever could.

Did you know He has your picture in His wallet?

He takes it out and shows it to everyone. He is so proud of His favorite child.

Today, I am asking every parent who reads this article to do something important. Take a bar of soap or a tube of lipstick and write these words on your child's mirror: "I am Jesus's favorite child."

Every time you hold your child in your arms, have them look in the mirror. Then ask, "Who are you?" Teach them to respond with, "I am Jesus's favorite child." Affirm them by saying, "That's right, you are His favorite child."

I asked the young lady I met in McCloud to do this same thing when she went home. Every time she passes by the mirror and catches her reflection, she will remind herself that she is indeed Jesus' favorite child.

Today, you may be the one who needs that reminder. Whether you are a young person, a high school student, or an older person sitting in a retirement center, I want you to know that you (yes, you) are Jesus's favorite child.

Now, I want you to do something else. Read the following words aloud:

"I am Jesus's favorite child!"

When I remind myself who I am, the enemy has a harder time convincing me I am an orphan. Look into your children's eyes and remind them of their true identity today—before the enemy tells them something else.

Back 40 Ministries

Walker Moore has been in the ministry for more than forty-five years, the first twenty within the local church. For the past twenty-five years, he has served as president and founder of Awe Star Ministries, a rite of passage sending organization that, through the years, has equipped students to serve as adult missionaries in fifty-two countries. God has recently turned his heart from the international mission field to include the United States.

"Back 40" is a term he learned from his grandparents. The son of an Irish immigrant, his grandfather homesteaded several forty-acre sections of land. When Walker asked, "Where is Granddad?" the answer would almost always be the same: "He's out in the back 40," meaning, "He's out working a section of land."

Walker and his team are now working the Back 40, strengthening and refocusing churches in the United States and around the world. To see his parenting materials, including Rite of Passage Parenting and the Rite of Passage Parenting Workbook (for individual or group study), check out ropparenting.com. More of Walker's teaching and equipping material will soon be available for the local church.

To learn more about Back 40 Ministries, go to back40ministries.com.

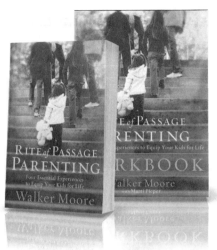

Rite of Passage Parenting

It's no secret: something has happened to America's families. Dramatic shifts in our culture mean that what was once an acceptable way to produce mature, capable adults has now all but disappeared. In Rite of Passage Parenting, family expert Walker Moore explains how that happened. And after concisely assessing the problem, Moore teaches you how to build into your children"s lives the essential experiences every child needs: (1) an authentic Rite of Passage, (2) Significant Tasks, (3) Logical Consequences, and (4) Grace Deposits from parents, grandparents, and other caring adults.

Walker Moore writes from years of experience as a minister, family speaker, youth culture specialist, and father. He knows well the damage to self-reliance, self-worth, values foundation, and identity that missing out on these essential experiences can cause. In Rite of Passage Parenting, he shows you how to prevent the damage and help your children move toward adulthood in a healthy way.

If you are concerned about the effects of the current cultural chaos; if you notice in your children a lack of responsibility, the lack of a good work ethic, disrespect for authority; if you are worried that your children may experiment with false rites of passage-profanity, smoking, drugs, alcohol, body piercing, or sex-let Walker Moore show you how to provide the four essential experiences most children are missing.

Go to Back40Ministry.com or WalkerMoore.org for more information.

Escape The Lie

When Jesus told His followers, I will not leave you as orphans. I will come to you. (John 14:18), He was referring to an ongoing relationship with a loving Father. But Satan s deceptive tactics block most Christians from the lives God intended. Escape the Lie: Journey to Freedom from the Orphan Heart uses powerful, biblical teaching about the three voices, identity in Christ, and the orphan heart along with compelling true-life examples to help readers identify and renounce the orphan heart s crippling wounds and move into abundant life. Walker Moore provides answers for the deep-seated problem known as the orphan heart. He also discusses the destruction brought by the orphan heart that dupes its unwitting host into a fatherless existence. He crafts a compelling analysis of the relationship God desires to have with each person that would set one free from the lies of Satan. This book consistently points readers toward hope in Christ and the freedom gained by overcoming the pain of our past.

Go to Back40Ministry.com or WalkerMoore.org for more information.

Inside Out & Backwards

If you enjoyed *Chicken Lips, Snake Legs & Jesus*, look for more stories of humor and hope, in *Inside Out and Backwards* coming this Fall.

Go to Back40Ministry.com or WalkerMoore.org for more information.